DANCING
DNA

DANCING
DNA

A COLLECTION OF POEMS

RICK ELLSMORE

DANCING DNA

Published by
Illumify Media Global
www.IllumifyMedia.com
"Let's bring your book to life!"

Paperback ISBN: 978-1-959099-41-3

Typeset by Art Innovations (http://artinnovations.in/)
Cover design by Debbie Lewis

Printed in the United States of America

Dedication

This book is dedicated to Lisa Hall, my one and only older sister. She has consistently been there, day or night, and has always believed in me. She has spoken of me being a hero in her life, well dearest one, you truly are a hero to me.

Lisa Hall and Jake Ellsmore, Knoxville, Maryland

CONTENTS

Foreword   xi

Acknowledgements   xiii

Introduction   xix

Part 1 Destruction

Introduction   2

1.   The First She   5
2.   Of the Wind   6
3.   Clown   7
4.   Tears   8
5.   Pain   10
6.   Trust?   12
7.   Red   15
8.   Wind   17
9.   Fear Is a Coward   19
10. Clinging   21
11. My Pain   22
12. Bedfellows   23
13. Forging   26
14. Drip   28
15. Back into the Now   29
16. Warring   32
17. Bridge   34
18. She Is Not Me   36
19. Letting Go   38
20. Diet Love   40
21. He Called Her Heaven   42
22. Game Point   44
23. Surviving   45
24. Maiden   47
25. Winning   50
26. The Box   51

27.	Intimate	53
28.	Hijacked	57
29.	Ripples	58
30.	The Color of Pain	60

Part 2 Awakening Through Courage

Introduction		66
31.	Boulder Beautiful	67
32.	Through Courage	69
33.	Emotional Sex	71
34.	Kiss of Presence	73
35.	Dragon's Fire	75
36.	Suicidal Keys	77
37.	Attacking Panic	78
38.	Effervescent Wave	80
39.	Glow	81
40.	Lovely	82
41.	Spirit Guiding	84
42.	Totems	86
43.	Firsts	88
44.	Exhilarating	89
45.	The Art of Life	90
46.	Lady of the Lake	92
47.	Ink	94
48.	Her Heart	96
49.	Home	97
50.	Searching for Words	99
51.	Spigot Hot or Cold?	101
52.	Beauty = Intimacy?	104
53.	Deep Roots	106
54.	Words	108
55.	Wu Wei	109
56.	Cream	112
57.	Calling us Home	113
58.	Long Haul Man	115
59.	Wet Ink	116
60.	The Fire of Her	118
61.	Lightning Kiss	120
62.	The Great Spirit	121

63.	The Way	123
64.	Beauty Bearers	125
65.	a sunflower she is	126
66.	Seeds	128

Part 3 Healing

Introduction		130
67.	Joy and Grief: Alive and Risking	131
68.	Why So Sad?	134
69.	Untethered Me	136
70.	On Fire	138
71.	The Warrior's Edge	139
72.	Liquid Love	141
73.	Becoming Love	143
74.	Ho'oponopono	144
75.	Dancing DNA	146
76.	The Edge	148
77.	Beauty so Deep	151
78.	Born to Wonder	153
79.	Reuniting Ancient Halls	155
80.	Intersection	157
81.	Build It	159
82.	her	161
83.	It's Beauty	162
84.	Back to Extremes	164
85.	Why Do I Write?	165

Part 4 Rebirth

Introduction		168
86.	Radiant	169
87.	Dance Yourself Clean	171
88.	-simple kiss-	173
89.	Tragical Romance	175
90.	Amazing You	177
91.	Comfort and Joy	178
92.	Knick-Knacks	179
93.	The Answer?	181
94.	The Sea	183
95.	Caught in a Moment	184

96. Ocean Blue 185
97. Lifetimes of Love 187
98. All… Is Poetry 190
99. We Scream; I Scream 191
100. Body Hatred 192
101. Want-Need-Deserve 196
102. Dancing Demons 198
103. Truth 200
104. Artistry 202
105. Rhythmic DNA 204
106. Given 206
107. Circles 207
108. Dressed in White 209
109. Found in the Echo 212
110. Richard Lee Ellsmore 214
111. Unrequited 216
112. Find A God Who Likes You 217
113. Giving of Fear 219
114. Two Wonderful-S 221
115. Never… (Ever) Enough 225
116. Universe Pouring 227
117. Hallowed Hall 229
118. Dancing with Desire 231
119. Getting Into Reality 233
120. Finally Home 235

About the Author 237

FOREWORD

By Rhoda (Rho) Resnick

Rick and I met in a funny way. I was standing in line at Lowes and got talking to this friendly man, Jiddi Shultz, in front of me. The subject of my flower garden came up, and I mentioned I needed a gardener as mine had retired. He mentioned that he had this super reliable man working for him named Rick. I gave him my number, and Rick called me the next day.

Our first meeting was outside in my garden, which was ostensibly to discuss all the work I needed to have done. Three hours later we hadn't mentioned work, but our bond was sealed despite the thirty years difference in our ages. We have been sharing in his poetry since our eyes first touched each other.

Rick's poetry is like opening a treasure book. Each poem is so intimate; it's so soft and loving. Then boom! You'll be hit with a line that will go, "Oh, that hurts or that must have been a really difficult place." His poetry is different from any other poetry I've read. It's like a constant stream of water that just goes and goes and sometimes slows and then goes again. There is a control in the midst of all that emotion and what he is searching for in his words. His ability to see and analyze many angles takes me on a journey with him through it all.

I sometimes feel like I am sitting on a mountaintop and just saying, "Oh, I understand, because I have experienced many of the same emotions and experiences." It's a rare gift to share this level of depth without having to state right or wrong answers and to do this through questions and experiences in the moment.

Rick has had great sorrow for a long period of his life. Not anymore. Now it's open. The door has swung wide, welcoming in joy, laughter, beauty, and love. His poetry comes pouring out directly from his soul. I've personally witnessed him beautifully emerging. It's been joyful for me. Rick has given me an enormous gift in allowing me to explore by his side. I celebrate our deep friendship and the magical bond we share.

Rho & Rick at the Colorado Symphony, Denver, Colorado

ACKNOWLEDGEMENTS

There was a time when my future teetered between life and death. A period I chose to get help and commit to a process that continues to this very day—to seek healing with tenacity and purpose. Over these past twenty-five years, I have had the most amazing friends enter my life. The width and depth of the love that has developed has, and does, reshape who I am. For a select few, they have become family, and their love and kindness are imprinted into the words written in these following pages.

During this time, I have learned a lot about the emotion of gratitude. For me it's a way of showing kindness to a person or persons who have made a significant difference in who I am today.

As time has gone by, the importance of thanking people and putting words to my gratitude has become a priority. It is within this spirit that I have made it a priority to write a testament to who they are to me, and what impact their important role has played in my life. So here goes!

Erik James Ellsmore, Mitchell (Mitch) Grey Ellsmore, and Jakob (Jake) Merle Ellsmore, naming is important, and your names represent three of the most important men who have lived with me throughout my life. Having these young men in my life has helped to mold me into the man I am today. There is both joy and pain in our relationships, but my love for them has, and always will be, an integral part of who I am.

I wanted to say a special word about my relationship with Jake. This past Christmas he gave me a picture of the two of us inscribed with the words, "You are my hero." I look at these words daily as a reminder of who I am to him. He sees me as his hero, and in some ways having a son who believes this is the most important truth there can be. I am so proud of him and the person he is becoming.

Merle Engle, the namesake for my son Jake, there is so much to sum up into a short paragraph. We connected twenty-five years ago, and it didn't take long to realize he had more integrity than any other person I had ever met. Merle truly is my adopted father and continues to serve as a hero to me as I pattern my life after his honor, kindness, and love.

Mark Whitney, my best friend, there is no one on earth that I trust more than this amazing man. Mark's compassion and empathy for me, and for others, has served as a beacon that many times has brought me back to center when it was desperately needed.

Jon Huerta, my fourth son, has brought so much truth into my life. Someday I believe we will pen a book together describing the incredible way we connected and the journey that has been our relationship. I beam with pride in seeing how much this amazing man has grown and is courageously stepping into himself.

Rhoda Resnick, or Rho as I and so many others call her, has been the supercharger that has vaulted me forward into discovering more of myself. A part of me refers to her as my mom, yet it is more than that. She has a zest for life and a love for her family and friends that has brought a deep richness. She is both a cheerleader for "team Rick" and one of my best friends. The time spent reading and talking through my poetry have been some of the most meaningful hours of my life.

Gray Le Master, the namesake for my middle son, was the first person I ever trusted enough to open up about my childhood abuse. We spent two years together, and session by session he helped to bring me back from the dead. His intense belief in me, and extreme honesty, continue to serve as a model of how I love people to this day.

John Kriz is my dear friend. Interesting fact, my fourth son's middle name would have been "John," and look who I "adopted" as my fourth son, Jon Huerta. Twenty-five years ago, he believed in me and that belief continues to this very day. His compassion and love for others continues to be a model of how I want to live by loving others.

Kim Brewer, this amazing woman, entered my life as a whirlwind and this energy continues to this day. She and her two lovely daughters, Lei and Kiera, have brought nothing but joy and beauty—well and maybe some crazy-fun laughter. During the darkest of my times, Kim and I would meet for lunch every week and talk through it all. Oh, the stories we have to tell of our adventures together! There is nothing I wouldn't do for these three lovelies.

Andy Garner, it's impossible to put into words what his friendship and love have meant. Throughout these past six years, he has walked beside me every step of the way. His belief in me has never wavered. He has shown up over and over to be in my corner and stand up beside me. I have such deep respect and love for him.

When I think of Don Rickard, *joy* is the word that comes to mind. My friendship with Don has been one that holds complete honesty and truth. I have never walked away from our time together not encouraged. In my darkest times, he has been someone who has had the capacity to walk with me there and provide the needed space to hold who I am.

Scott Jenkins, his coming into my life was like a slow developing thunderstorm. It brought a revolution of thinking and was what I needed to move into the next stage of my growth. I remember him saying at our first coffee together, "Your wife is going to hate me," and thinking it was an odd thing to say. Now I get it, and have repeated those words to men I've connected with as well. Scott is a trusted friend, and my deep appreciation and love for him has never wavered.

Orpha Fiona Mwende, my adopted African daughter. What a joy she has brought into my life. Her wisdom and integrity continue to amaze me. Her grit in dealing with her life in Kenya has been a model that has called me back to my truth. She has become such a treasured gift!

Stacy Landon, her guidance as a counselor has been part of the root system that has held me together. She has been both cheerleader and guiding light as I have found myself lost within the dark caves of these past six years. I can always count on her absolute honesty and quick wit to call me back to reality. What a gift she has been.

Gillian Tracey Scott, in a short amount of time, she became a muse, best friend, and a person with whom I entrusted my heart. Her warmth, spoken with a British accent, has forever changed me. She lives with a contagious fire, a fierce spirit, and an elegance that charmed me beyond words. Her coming drew forth a new depth within my poetry.

I want to thank my younger sister, Amy, for her belief in me. Chris Bason for over thirty years of friendship; Charlie DeMarco, for the amazing empathy you have always shown; Clark family, for embracing me and my boys through the years; Kevin Huff for the two years we spent meeting at the Oasis; Mark Schatzman, for believing in me when I most needed it; and Faith Donaldson, for helping me to see, experience, and start healing my feminine wounding.

I thank the woman I have dated over these past five years and the few that still hold a special place in my heart. You are each represented within the preceding poems.

Lastly, I thank my parents, Jim and Sarah Ellsmore, for their part in my entry into this world.

INTRODUCTION

The wind spoke to me. I remember the day, the time, the moment, and the exact spot on the NCAR Trail in Boulder, Colorado, when I heard her voice. Sacred and smooth, vibrant and fierce. My arms flew open, my mouth automatically went agape as I allowed her spirit to consume me. It was in this moment that I felt the beginning, whenever and wherever that was. The reality was that I was breathing the same air as all others before me have breathed. I knew this moment was forever changing something within. I silently stood, oblivious to other hikers, and I welcomed them.

I find myself hiking within the Rocky Mountains whenever I am able. It's a ritual I have developed, choosing the exact hiking spot to meet me emotionally where I am at on that day. As I move, I feel. When moving during the day, I allow the spectacular sun, and his masculine energy and light, to pour upon my exposed skin. If I'm disappearing into the night, I welcome home the moon and her delightful effervescent beams deep into my being. Their intimate touch is like no other—inviting their healing power as I gaze up into their illustrious warmth.

I've learned to allow my senses to serve as a bridge, awakening the ancient DNA inside. The smell of dense earth and spring flowers on the edge of blooming; feeling the roots of an Aspen grove alive underneath. The rugged pine as they tenaciously stand erect, meeting the mountain air. The chirping of birds, the chatter of squirrels, the thumping of woodpeckers, all these sounds resetting the rhythm of my being. The touch of the rocks, their ageless energy filling me while calling out to me to surrender within the beauty that surrounds. There is a recalibration taking place with every step.

As I spend time with my amazing friends, my family, these deep connecting moments call me back while encouraging me to connect into the moment and allow the depth of our mutual love to heal. Drawing forth a flow from my roots, the pieces of me found deep within the earth. As I sit in the presence of intimate love and gaze upon a lover, she, Mother Earth, the only woman I see. Our fingers dance in delight as one simple touch calls us into the divine truth of the moment. The fire burning in our eyes exclusively for each other, a silent whisper drawing us up into the sacredness that love is designed to be.

It's within these stunning moments, and others within my day, that my DNA is found dancing. This amazing understanding showing up like puzzle pieces over these past six years. The phrase *"Dancing DNA"* first popping into my being (yes, words continuously pop in!) on November 17, 2020. That was when I wrote my first poem about this concept that I had felt my entire adult life.

I believe I became an adult at twelve years old. I awakened one day to an understanding, an awareness of good and evil, seeing the light and dark playing out within my family and the community in which I was raised. This understanding of what I now call Spirit or Love was always there, even in the darkest of times.

This collection of poems, what I call my autobiographical poetry, is my journey through coming to terms with this place within myself. It's a reflection of my journey toward finding the courage to truly accept and learning to love myself—and discovering that my real name is RLove. That, in fact, I am, and we are all, Love. It is hope, joy, pain, and fear that make up the foundation, calling us into beauty; it's within this holy place that we are welcomed into the intimacy of Love. This is Dancing DNA.

A few years ago, a friend shared the Japanese concept of *akai ito* with me. The reality that there is a divine "red thread" that connects all of time—everything, everyone to each other. This new understanding brought me into the world of Allan Watts, who speaks so eloquently of the *wu wei*, the reality that everything, like wood, has a grain or rhythm to it. When we slow down and live within the gift of the moment, we experience the essence of time. And in fact, we control time versus being enslaved to its endless ticking.

My highest hope is that there will be something in my writings that will speak to you, that will be a salve within your darkest of wounds and life experiences. I hope that like me, you will find new places to dance, to celebrate within this life you've been gifted. Within the freedom of dancing, you will experience the inner awe and wonder of the child wanting so beautifully to come alive.

At any point you would like to talk about or share your experiences with my poems, never hesitate to reach out. I would be honored to receive your words.

Rick/Richard Lee/RLove Ellsmore
720.810.2124
searchfbeauty@gmail.com
https://rickellsmore.com/

PART 1

DESTRUCTION

INTRODUCTION

The first part of this book is titled "Destruction" for a reason. The year 2017 brought one traumatic wave after another. Each one adding to the misery felt within the one that preceded it. This tropical storm of a year brought poetry with it. My first poem popped out on an early spring day:

Spring Birds
The sunrise spring birds sing their tunes.
Never alone they worship joyfully.
A song to be shared with and by all.
A hymn to honor the spectacular earth that is ours.
My early morning heart dancing a jig to the good vibrations.

Nothing spectacular. A poem savant I was not. But I had done it. Somehow crossing a threshold for the first time, I started writing every day, putting words to what I was feeling and the onslaught of pain.

The month before I wrote this my grandmother, Ella West Ellsmore, passed away at the age of 103. She was a beautiful, kind woman who carried herself with grace. She lived a simple life, walking and painting almost every day—ending up with thousands of paintings and painted rocks. I directly connect my sensitivity into the beauty of who she was.

Three months later, and three days before Mother's Day in 2017, I received a call that my mom would not survive more than

2

twenty-four hours. I bought a ticket and flew into Pittsburg to be there and say goodbye. Her viewing was on Mother's Day, and I wrote a poem each day of that month. It was during this horrific time that I started to realize how poetry could help me through these painful losses.

That was the year that kept on giving—and not in a good way! The heartbreak refused to stop. It was as if a spigot had opened, and the valve had somehow broken. No matter what I tried, my life seemed to unravel more and more. My marriage of twenty-seven years (thirty-two years together) ended in a horrific way, and a month after that, I lost my Aunt Jean, with whom I had grown very close. Yes, she was the third woman in my family to die in nine months. I had two deaths in my neighborhood that finished out the year in a horrid way. After five physical deaths and the death of my marriage, I was a walking zombie. My life had dissolved before my eyes, but I was left with a few important things. I had a group of close friends who loved me. I had an inner tenacity that said I would not give up. And I had my writing.

Around that time I asked a dear friend, Lexanne Leonard, if she would read some of my poetry and offer her insight. She helped me refine my work and also invited me to her writing group of more than ten other fabulous writers. It was during these months that my writing started to blossom. I'm indebted to her and the gift she has been.

Part 1 of this book catalogs the darkness and light I was experiencing on a moment-by-moment basis April 2017 through October 2018. Every poem within these pages is in chronological order. I wanted to document the process of life as I knew it being stripped away, and being built back up.

The First She

*This was the first time in my life that I referred
to God as female.*

Her playfulness | Causing deep amazement
    Her laughter | Bringing a sizzle of life in the air
        Her smile | Vibrantly glowing onto all of the earth
            Her simplest movement | Arousing a deep
            longing
        Heart, mind, and loins | Feeling Her presence
She, God | Is like no other

"Playful Feet," Boulder, Colorado

Of the Wind

Mother's Day 2017,
the day of my mom's viewing.

I am a gypsy
Made
     of
       the
         wind
A traveler within t i m e
An animal
Flying
     in
       the
        sky
Not letting the grass grow under my feet
Needing to move, to grow, to change
Shedding my skin
Tilling the soil of new life
Planting new s e e d s and watching them grow
I am a gypsy
Made
     to
       glide
        in
         the
          sky

Clown

Like seeing a clown on a misty night

> What a terrifying thing
> It is to be myself in
> This moment

Why?

> Because I am
> A haunted house

TEARS

⊢────────⊣

This came from an experience I had working at a children's hospital.

Walking through the hospital today
A young couple wept
Clinging to each other
Tears streamed down their faces
Eyes tightly closed
Holding a tiny bundle of life in their hands
The blanket showing pink beneath their arms
Everything in me wanting to hug them and share tears
What had been said?
What lies ahead for them?
This was a moment in their world of time
Never forgotten
Played over and over again

Lumbering away
Mesmerized by the blink of their life I witnessed
I sit, weighted down by their beautiful pain

"Lonely," Stanley Lake, Colorado

Pain

*I was listening to Johnny Cash's version of Trent Reznor's song "Hurt"
as I wrote this poem.*

PAIN.

Flooding my system | I'm immobilized | A rat in a trap
Squirming to find release | Caught

PAIN.

Restricting my ability to be free | Locked in place
Feral in despair
Body swelling up | Expanding from this tourniquet of torment

PAIN.

Forced inside me | Imprisoning me | Tormenting me with its
relentless cries
Irrational in desperation | *When will it end?*

PAIN.

"Battlefield Trail," Gettysburg, Pennsylvania

Trust?

SPOKEN WORDS

"Trust me" | They say empathetically | *"Stop crying. Quit whining. Suck it up."*
"You lied to me" | Yelling | *"This will teach you not to wet your bed"*
"You kids! It's your fault" | Hissing out in gulps | *"Go to bed'*
"Lay still while I spank (beat) you" | Vigorously forced out
"We do everything out of love" | *"Jesus loves good little boys"*
"We're your parents and we know what's best for you"

EARLY TRAINING

They were not to be trusted | Never caring what was best for *me*
Like a beat dog, I tried to please | Desiring affirming words and the touch of love
The same wretched record played every day | Nauseating tunes brainwashing *me*
12 schools in 12 years | Dangerous environments with untrustworthy people
Awaiting each change | Controlling, abusive, and evil people
Those who lived by the "rod" | Maiming and killing innocence with a double-bladed "sword"
My parents' house was not a home | It was a prison | Imprisoning the real *me*
Raping innocence at every turn

My core memories are profoundly negative | Crumbs not equaling
enough to feed a mouse
Bouncing around my brain and hard-wired | Now clinging to the
fact I made it

SURVIVAL

Seeing strength in survival | I survived, understanding I didn't
succumb
Escaping the wretched belief system | Getting out at 15
Choosing an existence without them
Untrustworthy is one of my core memories | Unsafe to be *me*
Bumbly, goofy, and often, effeminate, *me*
Learning at an early age my "feminine" emotions had to die
It was up to *me* | To protect *me* from the monsters
To insulate *me* from everything in my world
Hiding in books, music, and the fantasies of being loved
I now understand as an adult I've often felt unsafe
Crevices within dark pain too difficult to allow trust to enter
Learning to hide the real *me* behind grit, quiet, and pain
I have felt this within my relationships | Feelings of being
abandoned
An erosion of trust | A disheartening presence within my marriage
Not believing I can trust love with the real *me*

TRUSTING

I'm learning to trust more of *me*, with others
Sharing more of my inner thoughts, struggles, and joy
It's a scary proposition | Sharing the real *me*

I have a lot to learn in this trusting area | Discovering the real *me*
The puzzle pieces still being linked together
Courage nudging me forward
Tenacity is a welcomed soulmate | Joy hard to come by
Slowly dawdling in
This raw place filling with tender feminine and masculine love
Morphing into one that is blossoming in its zest for life's essence
A place that advances me closer to loving *me*
No longer defined by their untrustworthiness
The trustworthiness of myself and others
Becoming the new *me*

Red

Red crossed my path | Red the Red Fox
Residing in a den | Close to my home
Glimpsing before but never like this
Rounding the corner | The sky lightly spitting
Morning haze encompassing | My presence known
Well before crossing paths
Red gazing over a long narrow snout | Eyes locking
Lasting a couple of seconds

What an instant it was | Slinking away
A blur of white from a paint brush tail
What splendor | Found in this wild creature
Often seen as a nuisance | Not I

The Celts believed the fox was a guide | Offering wisdom
Observing much | Wily intelligence
Worthy of honor | Seeing Red this day is timely
Guidance is needed as I foray forward
Knowing the fox relies on whiskers
On all legs to navigate the dark

The unexplored consuming my thoughts
Stepping deeper towards a new breath | Embracing the fear
Anxiety breeding within

I've heard an Irish Proverb say, "The fox never found a better
messenger than himself"
I'm thankful Red follows those keen instincts
I have deep appreciation for the "Reds"
The select few pointing out the landmarks
Unsparingly giving | Their tale on full display
Admiration burns for these treasured friends
Accompanying adopted family
Blood
Red continuing
To show me the mystifying way

"Running Fox," The Addiction Tattoo Shop,
Aurora, Colorado

WIND

Sitting | Air cool | Thick with motion
Aware of the warmth floating above
Conflict forms the enveloping fog
Bones hardened from the cold
It vigorously pursues
Ever aware of the wind
Why do we believe in the wind?
The surrounding reality
Proving existence
Yet feelings can negate

The wind
Moving unabated
Wildly seeking
Fierce in its non-surrender
Holding intimately to this fact
Attuning to the knowledge of belief
Wind is there | Unseen | Felt nonetheless

"Floating," Stanley Lake, Westminster, Colorado

Fear Is a Coward

F-E-A-R

Dominating in its presence | A ghost in the night
Grinning incessantly | Void of distinction
Heavy in personhood
Making aware danger and hazard | Shouting in my brain
Thieving joy | Weighing down while weakness sprouts
Suffocating anxiety | Controlling every move
A pulsating vile coward

F-E-A-R

Living with belief the cold shoulder would work
Ignoring at every turn | Avoiding in anxiety's wave
Failing miserably | Told it's only godly to fear God
Not anything or anyone else | Shamed for being fearful

F-E-A-R

A new realizing | Fear is required to survive
What would happen if "fear" received an Evite
A welcomed guest at an uneasy table | No avoidance
Facing fear eye to eye | A stare down of sorts
A light pops on | The more embraced
The more movement to beyond | Experiencing freedom
I wonder | Clearing out the haunted within

F-E-A-R

Is fear the coward? | *Am I the coward?* | It can be both
It can be neither | Often a combo deal | It's normalized
Fear is common to everybody | Every mind | Often hidden
Some scaling the fear mountain higher | Striving into
Out of bondage | A changing stance for fear
A serious scowl | Be aware | *Beware* of danger | Neutral
No judgment | Doing the job meant to do
No longer fearing fear | Moving forward into my future

"Darkness Within," Arvada, Colorado

Clinging

Written for my grandmother Ella West Ellsmore.

Clinging desperately | Safe in her tree
Limbs extension | Offering life-long grip
Wind blowing to and fro | Terrors' reign
On the ground | Seen from above | *Can she let go?*
She dangles | Alone | Abandoning family | Friends departing
Floating to the ground | Browning | Shriveling | Crumbling
back into earth | Courage needed | In fears insidious face
Releasing the death grip | Believing in the circle
Offering hope | Opportunity | In death
A letting go | For herself
For others
Her family's survival
Seeded by courage | To release | And contour
Through time | Welcoming generations | Embracing fate
Allowing for freedom's sake | Let go & trust | New creation awaits

My Pain

Please understand and remember
    My pain is *my* pain

You are not my pain
        Some actions and words
        Have caused a piece of *my* pain

Actions, words, or emotions
        Are not us
        They are not who you are
        They are not who I am

Remember
        My pain is my pain
        You are not *my* pain

BEDFELLOWS

$$\vdash\!\!\!-\!\!\!-\!\!\!-\!\!\!\dashv$$

"Fate is a fickle mistress; destiny is a whore."
Not sure who first said it | It's been heard nonetheless
Why do many negative things end up being female in nature?
Unfortunate | But expected
Anyways | Fate | Seemingly undependable and inconsistent
What and *why* immediately come to mind | It's talked about
Thought about | Written about | Stressed about | Endlessly
The never-ending questions | Propelling us onward
Or cementing us in place

"Fate is willing to do anything to get her way." (Anonymous)
Can we argue with this fact? | We have no control
Famous people guide our thoughts | Of new | And old

"Thy fate is the common fate of all; into each life some rain must
fall."
(Henry Wadsworth Longfellow) | *Could it be that simple?*
Must we just accept? | The reality | Shit happens | To us all

"Man does not control his fate. The women in his life do that for
him."
(Groucho Marx)
Familiar quotes | Fundamentally inherent in our
language | We laugh | In our laughter | We hide
Instilling blame | Avoiding the internal wrestling match

23

"Fate gives you the finger and you accept." (William Shatner)
I'm sure Captain Kirk means his middle one | Fate is
The divine screwer | Of one | Of all | Many believe

"Our fate is determined by how far we are prepared to push ourselves
to stay alive—the decision we make to survive. We must do whatever
it takes to endure and make it through alive." (Bear Grylls)
Pushing through | Defines our fate | A survivor's mandate
I understand

"These clashes are the only evolu-tionary possibility which will enable
us one day, now that Fate has given us the Fuehrer Adolf Hitler, to
create the German Reich." Henrich Himmler
Fate is manipulated | Beyond words | Blamed for atrocity
Devastating societies | Becoming whatever needed
Serving twisted evil

"There is a Grand Designer behind everything. Your life is not a result
of random chance, fate, or luck. There is a master plan. History is His
story. God is pulling the strings." (Rick Warren)
God is in control | There is no fate | A master of puppets
Pulling strings | Widely believed

Paulo Coelho writes, *"I can control my destiny, but not my fate."*
Profound words | In his simple complexity | He goes on
Not abandoning | With just those words

"Destiny means there are opportunities to turn right or left, but fate is
a one-way street."
Now this is something | Resonating deep within | A way

To not allow | The uncontrollable | Next moment to dominate |
Focusing my aim | On what I can control | My choices now
Within this moment

Can peace live?
Without full understanding | Trusting ourselves
Trusting an eternal guidance | Eternal love
My new t-shirt will read | Fate Happens, embrace it, move on.
It's uncontrollable!
Strive for a new now… your destiny.

"Fate loves the fearless." (James Russell Lowell)

"Walking the Line," White Ranch East Park
in Golden, Colorado

Forging

It was two years ago | Exactly
A new trail illuminating itself
I didn't plan it
       Didn't know where it was taking me
In these past months
      Death has been found
      Despair
      Depression
      Pain
      Loss
      Fear

I've experienced | Newness | Moments of joy
Breathing alive | Tasting an invitation | To a banquet table
I'm learning to see better | Listen more fully | Stop and not just
Smell the roses | But write about them | And take a picture
I've learned the grinding must stop | Otherwise I will be ground
to nothing | Pulverized like corn on a mill's stone wheel

I've learned | The value of real friends
Tasting of an ice-cold drink | After an 8mile hike
Offering life | Gifting understanding | I'm learning
What I have to offer

The unique piece shared | With those close to me
I've learned that no matter what happens
I will survive | That is what I do | Always have
Always will | I can't give up | On me

Drip

I drip | Blood flowing | Burning bright onto the paper
Bleeding through | Melding dark within the grain
Discoloration | Spilling over the edge
The floor its ultimate victim

My heart | Like a fish | Thrown out of water
Flopping around | Bouncing off icy cold tiles
Gasping for breath | The open wound
Raw | Aggressively pooling
Strained by unending
P-A-I-N

My words | Pouring out in my mind | From my soul
Bursting like a dam

A tourniquet | Halting the bloodletting | If only for a moment
A savior | Offering hope | A scab | Naturally forming
A scar | Leading the way | A healing
Peaceful Spirit

Back into the Now

My pain

My misery

My loneliness   Continuing to grow

Spreading like the flu   Becoming airborne

Viciously alive

Moving from my head   To my heart

To my soul   To every part

                        Of my being

Trying to cause paralysis | Gangrene wanting to form

A desire to give up | Giving into the darkness

Refusing | Putting my pain into words

Putting my anxiousness | Into pictures

Allow these new saviors | To keep me out of the pit

Sucking out rattler poison | Spitting in fear's face

I'm bleeding | Not dead

Wounded | Not giving up

The battle raging on | I will stay till the end

I can see the end in sight | The shoreline of home

Coming closer and closer | A place where I stand

Fate luring me forward | A siren to my soul

The mule satchels | Hung on a tree
Left behind | In the journey
For my destiny | For me | I move onward
Into the bright sun | With the moon's beam
On my aching back | Encouraging on by warmth
By light | By an internal guide | Letting me know
I'm not crazy | Or stupid | Nor am I unlovable | Or unable
To love another

The future calling me by name | I hear its melody in the fog
Tasting a time | On my parched lips | When the weight
Has been lifted |No longer do I carry | This weight
Of others | On my broken back

The path is laid out | Unchartered | In the course prairie grass
Air is ripe with destiny | Changing with every tiny step
A new tune | A beautiful ditty | Causing my toes to tap
my soul to leap

It's time
For the future
To live now | To breathe now | To experience now
To believe now | To walk now | To run now
Leaping towards the horizon
Anticipating joy | Peace
Awaiting as I move | From the desert
Into the spring fed new ground
I'm awakening | Into my heaven

"Into the Light," Platte River, Denver, Colorado

WARRING

———

It bloodies | Pushing from the inside | Raging loudly
Let me out | Wanting to feel the air | Anchored to the darkness
From which it thrives | Taking many forms | Evil anatomy
Maiming | At best | Destroying | At worst | Leaving behind
Sorrow | Grief | Probing agony

I've witnessed | Firsthand | The taking | Of a precious one
Young life | Vibrant and full | Before his time | A vial raping
Overtaking | A body | Ravaging flesh | Not spirit
Its randomness | Infuriates | Driving questions | Never wanted
To be spoken aloud | Desiring | Hurling back | Into hell's pit
From where | It was spawned

Learning to live | As pain's bedfellow | Facing death
Destruction | Knowing the fateful future | Is uncontrollable

Discovering | Living with this knowledge | Is a defining factor
Of who I am

"Sad Teddy," Westminster, Colorado

Bridge

The stones echo
    Footsteps shifting
      Toward the next
Time | Standing silent | Patiently waiting
Waters reflection | Capturing me | Dangling in between
Legs locking | Unable to move | From this moment

        The bridge | Stoic in form | Carrying my weight
        Simplicity | Burning through | My weary bones
        My wondering | Comforted | Rest Invited
        The Light | Burning red
        My essence alive | Inviting blue | Out into the open
        Comforting with yellow's hue
        Orange nudging me onward
        The journey | Awaiting on | The other side
        Inviting risk | Yelling freedom | Showing the way
        To life untethered

"Bridge Beauty," Flatirons Vista, Boulder, Colorado

She Is Not Me

She has | No control over me
Her attack | Does not define | What I need to do

Controlling

Who I am | Is often quiet | I overexplain
Due to fact | She likes me talking
Blaming me for being a control freak | Defining words
Float and shackle | Holding me down | Pummeling me
An insidious control

My quiet | Keeping me locked | Truth hidden
From illumination and light | My over explaining
A secondary friend | Used to fend off violent questioning
Put into play | To make me hate me

Common

These places | Common ground | From a time long ago
When the little one | Had his eyes burned out
A bridge | Connecting the worst | Of both worlds
She voices her heart | Hate burns deep
Constantly flowing her spin
Trying to make me believe | Her reflection | Poison mirror
Hiding the sickness within | Slowly taking control | Believing in
constant motives | Reflecting similar words spoken
To that little voice | So long ago

My childhood | Words were never enough | The true me
Never being enough for her | Often slamming the door
My living emotions | Defined by selfish gain
Cleaning out my closet | Showing me the need | To cull
Out the old

The overinflation | Of my being | The place ballooned
Quietness | Over explaining and fear | Making my clothing
Too large | Dead weight| Hanging loosely
My burdened shoulders | Weighing down
Anchored to pain | Sorrows wind

Process of Love

The process | Of true love | Kindness and empathy
Continues its foraging | Through me | Blazing a new path
One wrought with adventure | Exploring savage tundra
Lifting me up | My voice flying | Voices whispering | Truth
Love | Floating in fresh wind

Loving courage | Pulsating through | my hungry veins
I know now | Without a sliver | Of any doubt
She is not me | Just as I am not them
I am me | God is in me | I am in God | I am God
Formed from the eternal Essence

Letting Go

No control | Is being smashed | Deep inside
Crushing decades | Of corrosiveness
What can I control? | Is haunting question | From within

I can control no one
I can control no one's thoughts
I can control no one's actions
I can't control people's dislike of me
Nor their hate for me
If they love me
If they see me

Why?

They see | What they want to see
They listen to | What they want to hear
I can't control | Words | Actions | Betrayal
25% truths | Slicing deep | Into my aching veins

My choices
My actions
My steps
Are lighting up | As I work on | Doing the next best thing
And with that | Letting go | Of the belief | I'm in control

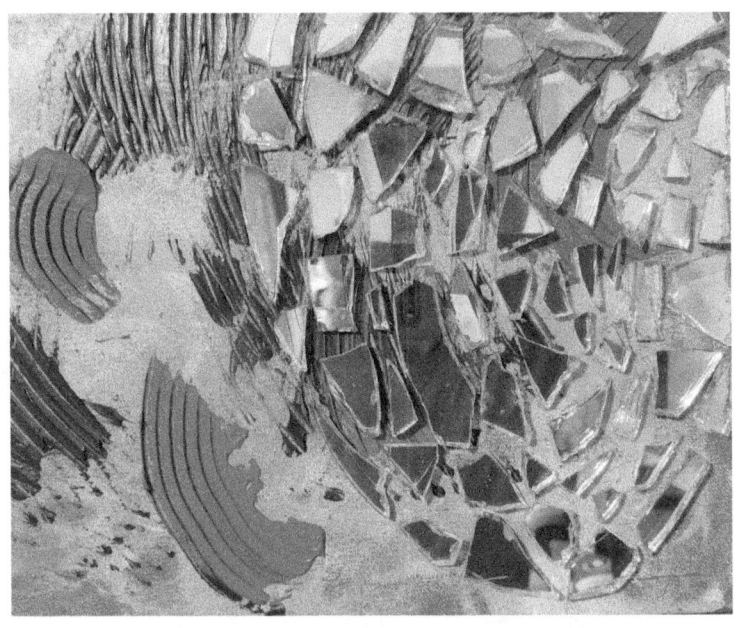

*"Broken Control," a piece of art I created hanging on my
wall in Westminster, Colorado*

DIET LOVE

———

You pop the top | The bubbling sounds
    Tickle your ears
        The anticipation
            Causing your mouth | To salivate
          Just the thought
              Upcoming sugar
             Sending great
        Vibrations
      To your needy brain
    Before you know it | It's in your hand
  Gulping down the hatch
The taste feeling so good | Down the throat

But wait

What is this shit?
    The aftertaste | Leaving your mouth stale
      DIET SODA?
        How did this happen?
      Oh, the insanity

          LOVE
          Have you
          Ever experienced
          Buyer's remorse?

You think

You are getting the real deal

Mexico cane sugar real

But wait | There is more

Does there have to be more?

Desiring the satisfaction

Of healthy love | Euphoria coming

With a long ahhh from your soul

A purr from your lips

Knowing you have been seen

Knowing you have seen

Experiencing joy

Titillation

Walking in rare air

Coming within

Intimate connection

He Called Her Heaven

Their brown eyes met | That split second
Is all it took | Realizing he would love
Protect | This little one
For her eternity
He instantly knew
He would walk | Over flaming coals
Swim an icy ocean | Step in front | Of a speeding bullet
Climb the tallest mountain | Walk away from his job
Heaven would know | No matter what

His daddy love
Would never go away
Would never change
It would always be there
During the darkest nights | On the brightest days
Little Heaven | Would somehow know
These truths

As she prematurely | Headed up to heaven
Awaiting his daddy love | To join her
Continuing the course
Permanently set
On this day

"Tiny Fingers," my great nephew, Lucas, Dover, Delaware

Game Point

I can't win
Which is ok
It's not about winning | Or losing

Why?

They will see | Fully understanding someday
Violent manipulation | Holding them down
Suffocating | A giant boa constrictor
Wrapping around their heart | Painful to witness
Excruciating in my helplessness

In the end
The light | Truth will shine
They will see | They will act
She will win| I will lose
The loneliness game

Surviving

Is surviving enough?
Your voice hasn't mattered
Innocence is stolen
Trust has been betrayed
You've been shit on
For the umteenth time

When *fuck* | Is the only word | Your ragged soul can utter
You persevere | Arising with the sun
Awakened toward a goal | A hope
Someday there will be freedom
Movement from the tyranny
So freely experiencing
You will survive
You will arise
Surviving
Victory

"Surviving/Thriving", Matthews/ Winters Park,
Golden, Colorado

MAIDEN

|——————|

There was a fair maiden | With golden locks
A sassy ass | She shined | She shimmered
She stole | The knight's heart

End of Hope

As a good knight | He tried everything
To win her vibrant heart
The quest took many years | Many mountains
Abandoning of identity
To please | To protect | To win | To be her one

The knight's quest | Took many turns
Many temptations | Persevering he did
Through many winters | Droughts
Never giving up hope
Until the end of hope found him

The Trap

The trap had been set
His every move watched | Every word analyzed
Poked and prodded
His past | Used as a skinning knife
Slicing humanity from his bones

Betrayal

He came in peace | Offering a drink
Offering understanding | To those sitting at the table
Before the cold liquid | Hit his tongue
The truth | Exploding his reality
Disintegrating disbelief | Shrouding his senses
How? | Why?
Words lost | In the cavern | Of his soul

The 25% truths | The lies | The poison
The vial betrayal | Spinning out of control
In an empty room | Glass all around
No longer veiled | Everything clearly seen
Denial and blame | Twisted fucked up game
Was played | Participated in
By those | He dearly loves

Reflecting

The knight | Sitting and resting
Dark warm liquid | In hand
Wondering within
What could have been done differently?
How could he have saved her?
Why wasn't his love, his sacrifice enough?

After many bloody battles | Far from home
Sitting in his wounds
Now understanding | He had fought | A winless battle

There is only one | Who could have saved her
Who can save her | It is not him

Lonely eyes bleeding | Salty tears
Foraging onward | Driven by the search

"Castle Shadows," Wawel Royal Castle, Krakow, Poland

Winning

Eyes burning red | Breath squeezing out
Disapproval apparent constant

           Can't win

           Couldn't win

           Won't win

           Done trying to win

She walks away | Feeling she won
Winning was never the objective | Her objective
She gets to live life | Knowing her choices
Gave her release from me | She won
Therefore, I win

The Box

The clouds ominously oversaw | Walking with another
Nine-year-old friend | A familiar path before us | A large box
Sitting alone | Stark in its contrast to the Alaskan nature
As young boys will do | We went investigating
Not ready to see | What was seen

Like the poisoned apple | I was drawn in
Blonde women | White and shining
Successfully selling their brand of femininity
Huge breasts | Strangely alluring
Flipping through the pages | Adrenaline pumping
So inviting | Stimulating the loneliness
The shaming overcoming | Winning out in the end

Running home | Distancing myself
From the danger exposed | The dirty felt
At such an early age | Spilling my guts
Through gushing tears
My father listened | No yelling
Surprisingly no judgment | Promising to take care of it
Promising Protection | Sleeping with mixed emotions
Breathing in the power of being honest
Breathing out the familiar shaming

Awakening to the new day
Walking the well-worn path | Alone
Expecting freedom | Anticipating fortification
The box sitting alone | In its exact spot

Wondering why | It lived another day
To echo its siren's call
The destroying of innocence
Allowed | Venomous through the veins
Why?
The Fearing of the box | Prevailed
My Mind acting | Robotic in its actions
Grabbing and running | Escaping the isolation
Hiding from the pain | Living in the secret
Feasting on plastic beauty | Stories implanted
Images ingrained | The box lid closed
On my young soul | Not knowing
It would be three years later | Before this stash
Would be | Left behind

"Grating Life," my kitchen in Westminster, Colorado

Intimate

⁓

Quick

Some down and dirty sex | Slam bam thank you mam
Or sir | Is welcomed | If desperate | Lasting sex
Is something desired | Quickies are a thrill
Often leave the soul empty
Tasting of cheese sticks
At Applebee's
Great going in
Going down
Void of sustenance
Leaving regret behind

Lasting

What is lasting sex? | 15 minutes?
An hour? | Three hours? | More?
This looks different | Based on where you're at
In the sex cycle | If you aren't getting any | Then 2- 5 minutes
Feeding the need | Often left wanting | 30 minutes seems great
What if you actually want more? | More than to "get off"
A desire burns | Not just in the loins | Deep down and core

Deep Yearning

Crying out from the beginning
To give | And get
To be seen | And to see
To desire | And be desired
To discover | And be discovered
To risk | And risked upon
To play | And be played with
To explore | And be explored
To invite inside | And be invited
To go wild | And be wild with
To drink | And be drank from
To celebrate | And be celebrated
To light the fire | And have flames stoked
Giving and getting | Getting and giving
This is a desire | My desire
More than just a quick fuck | More than just religious duty
More than just a need | More than just a spousal chore
More than just a partner's obligation | Embarking together
Finding a welcoming place | Bringing rest
Bringing understanding | Bringing a place of belonging
A trusting home | Safe to unpack | Safe to share
Foraging together through fear | In the end | Sex is not
The goal | The act is just the act | It's something deeper
The natural wanting to erupt | Orgasmic beauty awaiting
Spiritual | Emotional | Physical | Cosmic
A place of delicious intimacy | Exploring passions
Removing inhibitions | Experienced by few | Desired by many
Lusted upon by most | More than getting off | Or felt up

Unashamed

Is it possible to be naked and fully unashamed?
Physically naked? | Yes, we all have a birthday suit
Emotionally naked? | Difficult
Feeling no shame? | Damn near impossible
Thoughts creep in | Voices drumming from the past
Hidden fears awaken | You aren't beautiful
You aren't enough | You are a disappointing
You are disappointment
To fat | To skinny | Small penis | Small breasts
Scars | Stretch marks | Cellulite | Bald spot | No hair
To short | A big ass | No ass | A mid-section tire
OR, OR, OR
Our minds prattle on | Endlessly fine-tuning | Our faults
Exclusively focused | Even worse | Shamed by past experiences
Worse yet | Blaming ourselves | For being taken advantage of
Perversely used | In past abuses

Intimately Connecting

In the end | It is not about sex
But it is about sex | If you are understanding
Sex is all that | One with you | A reflective impression
Soul mate within | One that will not vanish

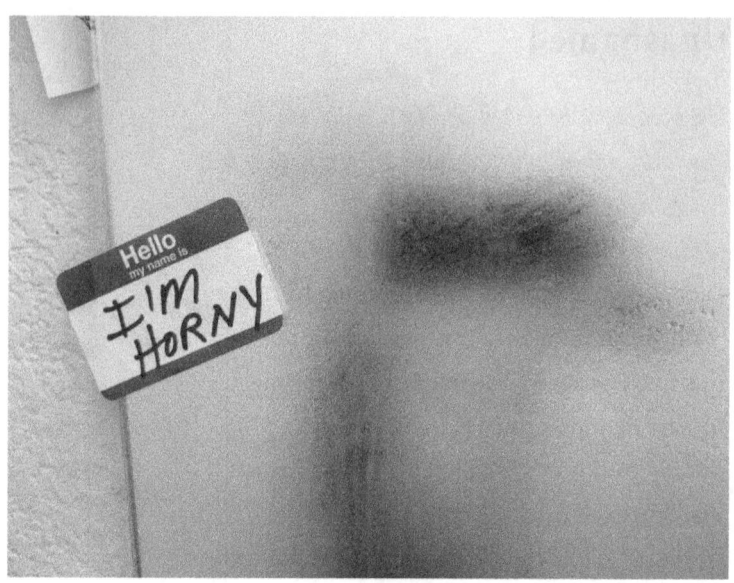

"I'm Horny," a drunk woman put this on my back
Northglenn, Colorado

HIJACKED

His pain
Hijacked by her pain
No more
Nothing fucking left
She stole it
He gave it away

*"Into the Dark," Boulder Library, Pearl Street,
Boulder, Colorado*

Ripples

Water rippling | Slowly moving | Quickly building
A small wave | Rapidly approaching
How had this started? | Am I alone?
Wondering if she was safe

Her feet pink from the water | Her toes numb from the cold
Her top hanging from the tree | About 10 feet away
Her black framed glasses | Sitting on top | Of muddy Nikes
Feeling naked and exposed | Just for a moment
The adventure | Accepted just this morning | Sitting at her desk

Bored shitless | Anxious for change | For once deciding to listen
That voice | The one screaming | R I S K | Step out
I AM a Colorado Girl | After all

This time she jumped | Mustang roaring | Heading west
Rocky Mountains swelling in size | Her favorite river
Loudly calling her name

Her beating heart | Settling down
It was only | A few rainbow trout | Swimming upstream
Spawning the next generation

The symbolism | Not lost on her | Sucking in
Deep thin air breaths | Her spirit | Leaping in delight
A fresh warm breeze | Gently pushing
Stress releasing from within | Into the awaiting water

No longer | Feeling naked | Or exposed
Breathing what felt like | The first time

The Color of Pain

Pain

Tattoo invited | Welcoming my guest
Yes | Crazy indeed

The title waves | Exploding skin raw | On fire
Bright red | Quickly bruising | First coating
Less than 24 hours old | Back-to-back days | Crazy me

Inviting darkness into my mind | Enchanting
Succulent beauty | The end result | On my ever-changing skin

Artist preparing | Her presence comforting
My trust unwavering | Hand steady
Gun engaged | Heavy metal laden inks
Orange and Atomic yellow | Pomegranate
Tahitian teal and royal blue
And of course | Power black

Readied | Operating magic | Smoothly shaven skin
Fearful but not afraid | Remembering paraphrased
Marcus Aurelius words | Puncturing my mind
It's not the pain itself, rather our fear of it

Growing Estimate

Nine round needles | Blazing the lines
Nine curved throwing shade | Hitting their mark
Needles puncturing | Over 2,500 times | In a minute
Endorphins exploding | Fireworks bolting
Willing veins accepting | Momentary high Toes squirming
Eyes closed | Earbuds loaded | Band selected

Killswitch Engage | Engaging and thrashing
The perfect notes | For an unsettled mind
Discomfort arriving | Cells rushing in
Trying to rescue | The foreign invade
Hitting the beach | Not boots | Ink instead

Stepping into a void | Perfect white | A presence felt
Beckoning inner shout |Trying to understand
Genderless | Only two beings alone | Unavoidable
Wanting to run | Eyes locking | The phantom in site

Seeing Closer

Expecting Jet black | Desiring black | But no
Dark blue presence | Midnight blue | To be exact

Inviting a response | Fear | Revulsion | Searching my mind
Desperate for a trap door | Waiting and patient | Knowing
The unavoidable | I return | Summoned by the voice

Pain speaks

Heavy in tone | Not scary | Power and full | Intensity growing
"Don't fear me, I'm not here to destroy" | *"Embrace me"*
Thoughts pouring in
Am I insane?
Why would I Embrace YOU?
The needle drilling deeper | Left arm's crease
Howling violently in desperation | The needles
Striking inner arm | Bile hitting my mouth
Piercing heat | Blowing through my bones
Screaming out an option | Putting an end
To this misery | Tempting me | Remembering

Knowing

Fully experiencing | Beauty means
Embracing pain
Only option | Natural action | Pain standing open
Accepting I move | Hugging my pain
Speaking, *"May I come in?"*
What? You want to come deeper?
My verbal thoughts
"You need to experience me From the inside out"
Nodding agreement | Swallowing my pain

The Entering

Electric zooming | Into my open mouth
Fully accepting | Feeling Neo like
After accepting the red pill

Pain speaking intimately | Engaged in my blood
The needle biting in deeper |Piercing unwilling flesh
"Embrace me" | Is what I heard | Louder
"EMBRACE ME!"
Tears flooding my eyes | Embracing my entire being
Every ounce | Every orifice | Allowing pain to possess
Peace and warmth | Mentally touching | Goosebumps
Muscles relaxing | Physically feeling every stroke
Every layer | My breathing | Back closer to normal

Welcoming

"Stop fighting" | Hearing over and over
Ringing in my ears
"I am not evil"
Reality of Pain's words | Stunning me

Entering different plane | State of being changed
"Embrace me" | "Accept me" | "Love me"
"As a part of you"

Words delivered from Pain
An unexpected intimate friend

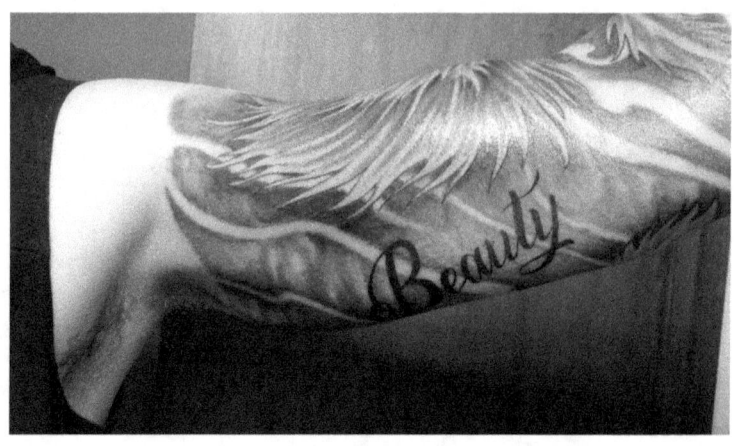

"Beautiful Pain," The Addiction Tattoo Shop,
Aurora, Colorado

AWAKENING THROUGH COURAGE

INTRODUCTION

Part 2 is titled Awakening because it was a season of waking up every single day and courageously moving into the day, facing ongoing issues. I discovered a tenacity I never knew existed within me and this is reflected within the following poems. The journey through this season, from November 2018 to August 2020, begins with a poem about stepping back into dating. My first date in more than thirty-two years. It didn't take long to discover how much I had to learn, and quite honestly, am continuing to learn.

The larger concepts I had been experiencing started to take root and have a permanent place within my daily thought process. An integral part of this process was discovering a depth of love I had not experienced before. I had moments of seeing my reflection in the eyes of another, which opened the door to the love I desired, both for myself and for and from another. The question, *what love do I deserve?* entered my consciousness.

Boulder Beautiful

Strolling in | Mudrocks restaurant name
Rolling around the brain
Promising myself | I would give this a chance
Understanding blind dates are hard
As if I was cold-calling on someone's door
The unknown of what's on the other side
Causing edgy emotions | Pushing out flooding red-faced fear

The first date | A year removed
The first, first date, in 30 years
They were sitting | Three people in a booth
Anticipating my entrance
Needing a fourth to complete the set

Wow | From a distant | Eyes met
A sly smile | Charging electric current
Into my brain | *This is who I'm here to meet?*
A space was left | A dazzling lady sitting alone
Not too close | Not too far
Introductions going well | A surprising comfort
A fifth person | At the table

Liking my choice in beer | Her classy tone
Piquing my interest
The evening | Like a blur | Fabulous and fluid

Unique moments| Laughter | Questions
All gathering tidbits of information | Moving towards a decision
Her piercing eyes searching | Trying to explore the inner me
Her intoxicating presence | Causing my system to overheat
Her Boulder beauty | Shining through

With more words spoken | Her friend | My friend
Giddy with delight | A second date planned | A goodbye hug
The physical connection | Getting the Oxytocin pumping
Confirming the obvious | Mysteriousness | Unique energy
Drawing me in | Another step | Being magnificently taken

"Blossoming," Back yard Sunflower, Westminster, Colorado

Through Courage

20 seconds | 60 seconds | 300 seconds
It's not the time spent | It's courage
The courage to step in | To move | To say
What you want to say | What you know
Needs to be said

To have a chance | To move beyond
A spark | Turning into flames
To speak | A gentle tenacity | Spoken

To invite connection | Intimacy
To listen to that voice | The flow of energy
That is whispering | Take a chance
Sometimes | It YELLS
Don't miss this opportunity

Courage | To find the feminine
I search for | I long for
Will only | Be found through courage
My courage to speak | To act
Her courage | To listen | And speak
Our trust

"Rocky Heights," James Peak, Colorado

Emotional Sex

She arrived a little late | How could I be angry
   She is so damn cute | And sincere in apologizing
She stands 5 feet and ¾ of an inch | According to her
   Her stature might be small | Her spirit is not
She is clearly a jean's girl | Her aqua scarf
   And other bright colors | Bringing out
Sparkling green hue | In her dazzling eyes
   She calls herself | Fun-sized | Sitting across the table
Experiencing her aura | I most certainly agree
   The rhythm | Instantaneous and exuberant
Conversation whizzing by | Bouncing from topic to topic
   Her simple way | Processing and describing life
Igniting my senses | Quickly discovering | A similar spoken
   Emotional language | You know that language
The one only you have | Or maybe you have a best friend
   That can speak it | Art, tiny houses, minimalizing
Her dreams for the future | Feeling goosebumps
   Running through the luscious fields
Of what could be
Over and hour has passed | A feeling rising
   Starting from my toes | Working their way up
No, I wasn't high | Well maybe on her presence
   How can I have so much desire for a woman I just met?

What a gift | To feel this desire | To feel her desire | For me
    Sitting in a restaurant | Picking at food
That doesn't matter | The most luxurious of meals
    Our clothes were on | I did not feel that way
It was if we were naked | Dancing in a fresh Colorado stream

KISS OF PRESENCE

⊢————⊣

I can rest | In the kiss of presence | In the present
    Having someone say and mean | I want you | To be you
        Don't hold back | Speak you | Live you | Feel you
        Be you
    A feminine delightful creature | Desiring me | As much as
I desire them | Feeling their zest for life | For me
    A woman | Who clearly longs | For me physically
        But lusts | My mind more
      This is not a normal thing | Women, well people, generally
Hold back | Reserving out of fear | Often out of wounding
    But not her | She is surprising | And thankful
        Appreciative of what I do | Why I do | How I do
    Her trust shocks me | Her history should not allow
This level of trust | *Why has she not run already?*
    My mind wonders | With all that's happened
        All that's been experienced | All that's been perpetrated
*How can I trust? | How can I allow a feminine spirit in this
place?*
She is not just any | I am not an ordinary person
    Who will never trust again

"Young Lovers," Pearl Street, Boulder, Colorado

Dragon's Fire

Used | Taken advantage of
Ignored | Neglected
Unseen | A dragon
In its egg | Kept present
Sleeping giant to be
A taste of freedom
Cracking the egg
Glimmer's of light seeping in
Freedom felt
Escaping the rules
Controlling personhood
Traveling 1000 miles away
Removed from the sickness
Only to discover
The dragon
Stays locked away
Unable to breathe fire
Under these familiar circumstances
Entering into a life
Starts and stop
Experiencing moments of fire
Only to be sucked | Back into the egg
Followed by | Loneliness and doubt
Three years ago | The egg cracking
Unable to piece | It back together

To fit back in | Tiny step by tiny step

The growing dragon | Physical
strength

Emotional depth | Stretching
bones

Underneath skin off steel | Built to
protect

Against the beating | Of the scary
Monsters abound

Searching for weakness | Wounding
Unable to destroy

The dragon's quest | For the fire to reign
Has not

Will not | Can not | Be halted

Instead he breathes | Alive and unstoppable

Causing fear

Uncomfortableness | In those not understanding

Disbelieving it can be real | He lives | He will continue

A fire burns | That will not | Can not | Be halted

Suicidal Keys

Keys in hand | Stinging cold | Oddly arousing
Potential opportunity dead ahead

Rest from the shadowing voices | The incessant ringing
Noon-bell at St. Annes

Keys to my future | Dense from the past | I'm sitting
What little there is left

Imagining flying alone | Escaping at about 100 mph
Right off the highway | A place where | The safety fence ends
Free air awaiting | My Supra | Red and ready
A willing participant | In my hands

Going out | In a blaze of glory | Floating together
If only for a few seconds | Settling into the inviting forest
Enveloping green | Hiding forever pain
Not to be discovered | At least for a while

Sitting on my steps | A crossroads | The past intersecting
Within the present | On the future's doorstep
It would be so easy | Feeling I would not
Ever be missed | In fact, my son | Better off without me

Sitting now | Typing these words | Wrestling with this memory
22 years | Thankful I didn't turn the key | Disappearing forever

Attacking Panic

The roar   Violently causing

Flooding through my system

My brain overloading   Heated within

Skin burning red

Unanticipated overloading   Thoughts running wild

Loosely holding on

A berserker hell bent   Havoc winning

How do I Stop this?

Quelling the fury   Embrace the panic

I've been told

Lurking behind   Allowing myself to grieve

The loss right under the surface

Inviting it to run its course   A new way of living

Allowing me to move along

Continuing my journey   Into the Light

"Lost in the Fog," White Ranch West Park, Golden, Colorado

EFFERVESCENT WAVE

A crescendo | Royal blue, teal, black, and white
Crashing into | Raging against | The awaiting shore
Causing shudders | Building and building | Fluid motion
The crescendo | At a fervent pitch | The switch flipped
Exploding joy | A mist of moisture | Raining down
Gushing wild | All over the awaiting shore
It's mouth | Open to receive | The incoming wave
Allowing its force | Enveloping it in a violent eruption
The shoreline | At peace | Savoring the outgoing tide

"Splash," Isabela, Puerto Rico

Glow

Her presence
Unlike anything experienced before
A woman
Yes, she is a woman | Mature and kind
Accomplished and sensual
She shines
Her desire to touch | To be close | Quite apparent
Her touch electric | Sending vibrations
Making my bones rattle | New energy seeping in
Her life fluid
Colors and beauty | Lighting the way
Her eyes dark | Deep and tearful
She is wanting to understand all that's happening
Attuned to wanting | To helping | To healing
Her story
Deep with pain | Enlighted by joy | Peace and time
Our friendship | Open and unknown | A thrilling adventure

Lovely

Her Spirit

        A butterfly

                Floating in the wind

She moves

        To the rhythm

                The earth's whisper

Magically pushing

        Her along

                Her breathing

                        Luscious with warmth

She sees

        She does

                She is

                    Lovely in all accord

"Italian Lady," Porto Ceresio, Italy

SPIRIT GUIDING

—————

She was dark | A Native of North America | Long and lean
Solid but yet | Smooth as silk | Coal black hair
Flowing in unison | Sleek body movements
Green glow | Activating magical
Within the gentle warm breeze
Shimmering rainbow bright
Senses awake
Kaleidoscopic colors
Left behind | As she is floating
Through the liquid air | Causing an effect
Similar to the contrails left behind | A jet engine In the sky
She doesn't speak | Lovingly inviting me inward
With the wave of a fluid hand | I went in
A spiritual day set aside | Exploring
The outreaches
Of an
Expanding mind
A fresh intention | To listen
Rather than to audibly speak | To be searched
Through silence | Rather than to search | Resting within
Versus actively looking | Physical eyes closing
Moments of darkness | Flying into my sight
Mediation moments | Infringing upon

The vibrant light | Overwhelming
Fear desirous | Complete focus
In the past
Fighting with all my might
Pushing out | Fear's intense | Weighty attack
A choice made | I will embrace it | Accepting its sticky hug
My Guide | Liquid Love | Leading me through
The thick black | Choosing the alternative
To see the Light | Found within
The dark | Not fearing
What is unseen
Embracing with |The knowing
The choosing to believe |She speaks
"Darkness is formed only because of the Light"
My journey | Trusting the feminine guide within
Moving the needle | Of my growth | Astroglide smooth
Serenely stepping | Trusting the quiet | Embracing the moment
This moment

"The Light," Stanley Lake, Westminster, Colorado

Totems

Pulsating | The energy field | Drawing me open
My essence on red alert | Sensing the welcoming wave
Intertwining connection

The mountainside | Luxurious green | The early rains
Bringing forth | Surprising Arizona spectacularness
Large families | Spiking the horizon | Banding together
In rugged force | These spiky sharp statues stand
Erect and strong

Guardians of their surroundings | Self-protecting
Small skewers sharpened | Awaiting any | Attack from
Human or animal alike | Slowly growing | In the dry
Barrenness desert hills | Inches creeping upwards
Some of these warriors | Two hundred plus years old

Totems | Large and small
Nourishing those around them
Their sap through drops of moisture | In the air
Their energy | Bouncing from one to the other

I stand | Their energy jolting | Inviting freshness
Into my malnourished soul | Thankful for their
Resonate strength

"Totem Power," Camelback Mountain, Phoenix, Arizona

Firsts

That feeling
When doing something | For the very first time
You know | A wild rush | Adrenaline pumping | Endorphins
gushing | In and through Your nervous system
Little Oompa Loompas Flushing chocolate
Down the hatch

What do you think of when you hear firsts?
First kiss | First date | First sexual experience
First roller coaster | First motorcycle | First pet

I remember | My first ride on my bike | Ending in a wild crash
The sidewalk getting the better of me | My first crush
My first love | My first great friend | My first pet
My first child | It's interesting
How negative
Positive experiences
Pop to the forefront of my mind
As I live in the present | More and more
What firsts Will I experience? | Allow myself to experience?
Will I look for them? | Risk moving towards them?
Allow them to infiltrate? And at times,
Be a course correction?

Living firsts | Truly is a way of life
Living like Jim Carrey in *Yes Man*
Continuing | To say yes
To firsts

Exhilarating

her eyelids
gently open
dark eyes
focusing solely
on me
taken aback
its within
a split second
i know
she can handle
the full me
i look back
i look within
not looking away
taking in
the deep reservoir
represented as I see
my reflection in her
connecting on a level
a dangerous
exhilarating level
wanting to know
this creature
To explore
frolicing
childlike as we laugh
tickle and play

THE ART OF LIFE

Blues, oranges, pinks | Flowing from the vast sky | Leaking
Beauty | Into the reflecting all around
The universe | Wrapping its arms around
Colors morphing into being
Deciding to fully embrace | This illustrious feeling
Setting off towards the place
Where sky meets the earth
A magical place | An enchanting moment
Coexisting together | Is not a pipedream
Rather, a reality
Entangling in love | Choosing presence
Desiring nothing more | Wanting only
For the wearied soul |To experience
Peace and rest | Feeling what it means
To be | Seen and loved | Rejuvenating
Acceptance | Enrapturing delight
Soul vibrating elation
Awakening the river within
Causing a gush of eternal movement
Readjusting the course of life | With the fresh waters guiding
The way into a new land | One aplenty with purpose
Lung-filling sighs | The flowing of childlike emotions
As if exiting from the womb | For the first time
Unexplored existence | Bubbling over

Cutting the cord | Into the way
Of the blues, oranges, and pinks

"Jungle Girl," Gia at Sunset Park, Westminster, Colorado

Lady of the Lake

Her presence | Living within
Blue green | Fully alive

The Lady | Welcoming my spirit | Into her world
Into a wild and vast dimension | Wooing me | To her
Water's edge | Wholly expecting | Water goddess
Ancient mermaid | To appear | Splashing ancient water
From time's beginning | On my sweaty face | On my
Art constructed forearms

I welcomed Her | Into the inner sanctum | Of my being
Wondering Her | Water's edge | Losing reality
For handfuls of spectacular moments | Resting in
Small, covered area | Gathering up small tokens
Rocks from her bosom | Sand from her essence
Ripping myself away | Traveling back
Walking the cobblestone | From Her | Beloved side
Transformed forever | Her Sirens song | Echoing within
The deep hollows | Of my renewing sanctuary

"Lady of the Lake", Czarny Staw Gasianicowy Lake, Poland

Ink

Ink | Meaning more | Then just adding
An "S" | Onto my I-N-K

Rearranging | S-K-I-N | To I-N-K | Forever resting
Inviting spirit higher | Your presence | Your kiss
Your love | A permanent sharpie | Imprinted upon
My flesh

Forever seeping | Deeply into | My lonely heart
Successively trickling | Into a cavernous well
Offering fresh water | Nourishing deadened roots
Back to life

Blossoming an aborted child | Lost long ago
Dripping ink | Inviting love's | Sweet taste
Onto my extended tongue

"Howling Flame," Addiction Tattoo, Aurora, Colorado

HER HEART

Her heart
　　Bathed in
　　　　The moons beam
　　　　　　Desperately clung
　　　　　　　　To his every
　　　　　　　　　　Seductive word
　　　　　　　　　　Her body
　　　　　　　　　　　　Shivering in
　　　　　　　　　　His presence
　　　　　　　　　Burning from
　　　　　　　　The volcano within
　　　　　　　Her lava
　　　　　　Red hot and fluid
　　　　　Freely poured out
　　　　Upon his awaiting heart
　　　Her lips | Parched with desire
　　Spread in the form of a circle
Whispering his name
　Upon the universal flow
　　Her fingers | Wet with the forest dew
　　　Calm and seductive | Lightly running
　　　　Up his chest | Alive with fury | Lust
　　　　Seeking their destination
　　　　His hot-pressed mouth

Home

An elusive word | Conjuring up many emotions
Filling minds | Smells. Sounds. Sights | From times
Gone by | Longing for more | Or whatever
This illustrious word | Home | Really means

Struggle

Witnessing so many | Struggle with the reality
They've never fully experienced a place | To fully let down
One filling with | Hope and kindness | Drawing out the
Poisonous venom within | Sorrow and loneliness
Unable to allow peace and joy | To settle in
Becoming the air breathed

Elusive

Home? | Emotions flooding | Writing this word
Pushing over | The top of my dam | Learning to allow
Them to have | Their way | No longer | Fiercely holding
The water's surge | From having | It's way

Child

As a child | Home was nowhere | Unable to find
House after house | School after school | Temporary toys
Temporary shit | Never settling | Long enough to experience
The warmth of home |Of community | Of family

Finding

Colorado has become | A place I call home | Never quite home
That small piece | Never fully letting go | Within my anxious
Unsettling system | In 2019 | Finding a place | Specifically alive
The fruit of | An arduous journey | Finally ripening
Experiencing a temple | Mystical and romantic | Found within
Going wherever I go | Peacefully settling in me

Enjoying the juice of home
As it runs down
A smiling happy mouth
Choosing to let it drip
Upon a graying hairy chin

"Home," Boulder, Colorado

Searching for Words

She said…
I love you
I love your words
I love feeling and knowing you through them

The Search

I've been searching a lifetime | For words | For my words
I look in nature | Looking under rocks | Looking in streams
Trying to hear in the wind | Nothing | More silence
Trying to talk | Literally opening my mouth
To have the words | I thought were there
Not bubbling to the surface | Frustration and anger
Becoming companions | Tearing into myself
What is wrong with me?
Knowing they are there somewhere
Not knowing how | To rip them out

Search is Over

I have found my words
They come out in writing | They are finally pouring out
Through a willing mouth | No longer having to rip and tear
Inviting them to the surface | Willing to allow their healing
Vibrations | To change who I am | Where I am going
Having one special and unique | Others taking my words in

Appreciating them | Encouraging more | More of me
Being discovered | One poem at a time

"Words Alive," Ghent, Belgium

Spigot Hot or Cold?

Is your spigot turned on or off? | Hot or cold?
Emotions | Difficult to talk about | Sometimes impossible
The experiencing | Often hiding underneath | Not knowing
How to properly allow | Tumultuous inner waves | To be seen
To be heard | Remembering a discussion | A young man
All ears | Wanting to understand | Why he was unable
To express | What was inside | Sharing with him
Our emotions | A knob | Turning water
Hot or cold | On or off | As kids
Especially boys | Raised to turn
Off our emotions
Or never allowing them
To turn on | Messages teaching
Importance of corking | Big boys don't cry
Crying is for girls | Be a man | Implying that it's never ok
To allow tears | Emotions | Through your internal pipeline
What happens when men don't allow their emotions to freely flow?
I remember the exact moment | Reaching the end
The Oscar winning movie | Moonlight
Playing out before me
Stoically sitting
Tears rolling gently

Down my cheeks | The main character
Born gentle | Kind and caring | Family and community
Hardening emotions | Mentally and physically |Beat out of him
In the end | As an adult | Coming to terms | The need | Urgent
Focused | To be seen | Touched and loved | A simple hug
Allowing freedom's gentle embrace | To be felt
As I look | The abrasive landscape
Violently alive in our country
Men lacking the ability
To emotionally feel
Showing up
At every turn
Anger and rage | Leading to violence
Blood stains unable to be washed away
Fathers handing down jail sentences | To our sons
For some | A life sentence | Trying to outrun | A father's legacy
For others | A life of loneliness | Enslaved to the experience
Escaping through addiction
What could be different?
What if our sons are gifted permission to cry?
Permission to express hurt and rage | Feelings within
Not treated as the enemy | Rather the way out
Of the immense pain felt
It starts | A simple message
Everyone is emotional | We all feel
These feelings are the placenta | Attached to us
Flowing from our mother's womb | For some | A lifeforce
Carried on throughout our childhood | For many | Violence
Severing | Treating us as soldiers | Needing to toughen up

The focus being the rough waters | Of life ahead
It's time to learn | Giving permission
To feel | In the moment |In doing so
Allowing those around us to feel
It's time to acknowledge
Other's emotions
With empathy
Looking beyond the rage
Trying to discover | What is backed up
Hair and black gunk in our pipes | Unable to be Let out
Let's be | Light-working plumbers
Gently unclogging
The growing pipes
Serving as revolutionaries
Drawing ourselves and those around us
Into deeper intimacy | Courageously transforming
Those we love and cherish

BEAUTY =
INTIMACY?

Rasping words | Ringing clean | Through my earbuds
Speaking about beauty | Beautiful playing out
Every moment | Through every outlet
Beauty is sold | Used to catch an eye
Capture a soul | The desire
Consuming | Playing out
One click at a time

What is behind the daily search for beauty?
Does beauty equal intimacy?

Or as Creed says, false beauty just leaves behind regret
Times in my life | Experiencing this | Regret myself
Tasting of imitation | Allowing its poison
To numb my need | For true relationship
Allowing it to serve as a roadblock
Keeping me from knowing
Deeper me | And another

Why do we humans move towards cheapened beauty?
Like a moth driven by light which is really lust?
Searching for more of ourselves

Settling for empty-calorie Twinkies
When we can experience homemade chocolate cake

Cheap beauty is a free commodity
Something that requires very little of ourselves
No giving or sharing | No stretching or growing
No facing fear that beads like sweat after a hot summer run

Intimacy is expensive
It requires investment | Requiring us to step
Out from the comfortable | Into the uncomfortable
Unknown | Being willing to face inner demons
Large and small | Risking a piece of ourselves with another

It's time to step | Time to expose our broken pieces
Allowing others a glimpse | The real you
Join me | In defying danger
Trusting another with ourselves
This intimacy
The truest of beauty

Deep Roots

Our roots deeply kept

Dark soil alive

Flags flying

Some people celebrating

Others cringing

Blood soaked

Ancient voices

Fighting for a land

Called home

Claiming freedom

At what cost?

Death and destruction

Of a way of life?

Often wondering

What if our ancestors

Had chosen another continent?

Would they be wiped out?

Slowly disintegrating

Where is my home?

Your home?

If not here

On this foreign soil

Then where Is home?

Discovering home

Found out there

Found in here

Accepting the reality

I am home

My ancestors

Belonging together

Not waving

A foreign flag

"Deeply Rooted," Palmas del Mar, Humacao, Puerto Rico

Words

Forever
  Echoing from galaxy to galaxy
    Wishing some could be taken back
      Others wanting to bounce around for eternity
    Written words
  Changing the way we do life
Impacting every meaningful relationship
  Forever changing in the reflecting clarity
    Brought forth
      Exploring the inner rim
  Of who we are
Who we desire to be

Wu Wei

The Chinese principle | Not forcing | Allowing natural action
Alan Watts says, "Acting in accordance with the
field of forces in which you find yourself."
My mind
Is captivating this thought | Different from the empty beliefs
Fashioned at a young age | Built upon | A limiting foundation
Searching and finding | Some similarity } More than
A play on words

One of Jesus' clearest and
Underdeveloped sayings,
"Become like a child."
To truly understand | How to live
Fall back | Into a place | Where fascination
Has a foothold within | Playfully embracing the present
Allowing time to stop | Within a moment | This moment
Turning 360 | Seeing every direction | Taking in as much
As can be seen

Last night | 5-year-old Gia | Running into the room,
"I have a nose." | Shouted out | With glee
My old adult mind saying | So what, it's just A nose
My more present | Childlike personhood saying
Wow, the nose is an Incredible thing |Think about it
For a second | Without a nose | Without smell
We miss | The delight found

In mouth-watering scrumptious foods
In a lover's Intimate musk
In the understanding
Coming from the simplest of smells

Let's learn | To embrace the world
The one around us | Truly being | Weird and wild
Living strange
Are we okay being strange? | Being a stranger?
Allowing the unknown | To draw us out
Not having it figured out | Mapped out | Planned out
Embracing the childlike mind | Without even knowing it
Choosing to be | In that energy

I have recently read | About ancient ships
2000-year-old sea-faring | Water plows
Discovering was found on the sea | Worlds expanding
Gliding upon | Her fluid motion | Different sized sailing vessels
Stepping into | The unknown | Facing fear and death
Man and nature connecting | Working together
Effortless movement | Using the wind
Shaping the discoveries found | In the unknown
Learning to not force | Movement forward
Rather to borrow upon | Her gracious gift
Imagining those | Water travelers | Sights seen
For the first time

I'm learning to not | Be aggressive
Or aggressively seek | The future
But yet | Not living in non-action
Or passivity | Words | Rhythmic and alive
Writing themselves | My sea-flowing outer shell
Inviting them forward | To have a voice

They often shape me | Not me shaping them
A learned place | Mind meditating | As they pour out
Flowing into my opening consciousness
I sit back in awe | At what they | Are wanting to say
Within me | Through me
Something I have been practicing | Starting 22 years ago
Not knowing I had been
Having to realize | I don't know | What I really want
Until quiet
Then I hear | My ears learning to listen
To that still quiet voice | I'm reborn
Coming again as a child | Allowing laughter
Surprise and kindness | To flow openly
With the energy | Of nature Herself

"She's In Motion," Mission Ballroom, Denver, Colorado

CREAM

ı———ıı

Creamy and extravagant
Smoothly it oozes
Allowing plenty of room
For temptation
Pure delight
Pure heavenly stream
Flowing from
The forest floor
Purified through
Natures illustrious moss
Overwhelmingly extravagant
Moving over
Into my senses
Causing a sugar high
Exploding sweet
Into my
Childlike
Exuberance

Oh how | She delights | Me

Calling us Home

A mountain breeze | Freshly moving through
The valley below | Bringing with it
An awakening | Within the essence
Of those willing to listen | Able to see
Ready to act | She is the pied piper
Playing Her siren's tune | An invitation
The young at heart | Ears to hear
Eyes to see | Nose to breath in
Hands to touch

Her Essence | Cast as a spell
Upon every simple moment | Her mist
A daily "dew" | Inviting adventuring
And firsts | Upon the day
Upon every day

"Walking Man," Stanley Lake, Westminster

Long Haul Man

Words popping | Into my liquid mind
A recent hike with a young man | Ever present
I'm not about going faster | I'm about going longer
Sharing the turtle analogy | Over-enthusiasm reigned in
Bullheadedness | Of no use | Pushing through everything
No longer desiring | The pain and loneliness | Coming with
This choice in life
Ahh, the wisdom of age | Wanting to go the distance | Farther
Than others | Before me | My lineage | Seeming to be able to go
No desire | To burn up to fast | Or to turn back
Out of exhaustion | Avoiding twisted & broken ankles
Choosing to plan appropriately | Focusing on the present
Therefore, tuned into the future | Accepting every step
Not hurrying the process | Quieting the little boy
In the backseat | Screaming, *When are we going to get there?*
 Slowly releasing | The red-face impatience | Fully taking in
The process involved | Embracing the journey
Encircling profoundness
Of just being

Wet Ink

Ink	Fingers
r	d
u	e
n	l
n	i
i	g
n	h
g	t

Her
wet
canvas

Alive
overflowing

With life-giving

ART

"Wet Beauty," Downtown Parker, Colorado

THE FIRE OF HER

She arrived quite suddenly
Moving in from east to west | Dry and bitter
Jumping on me | From the core | Of the mountain itself
Pelting exposed skin | Violently transforming | My budding
Expectations for the evening ahead

This moment | The very spot I stood | Would be one
Never forgotten| The night | She decided to leave

The day | Starting like | All the others | Radiant and blue
Welcoming me | With a bird's tune | A bee's hum
The Mother | Throwing open| Her loving arms
With every step | Of my La Sportiva hiking shoes

Like the brewing storm | Her energy shifting
The darkness | Showing up | Around her eyes
Squinting as she | Cut the vegetables | Standing next to me
Energy swirling within | Creeping its way down
Into her fervent lipsSeeing them | Starting to crouch together
Moving around like a rabbit | Ready to bolt
Into the awaiting brush | Seeping downward | Into her throat
I could envision | The boiling lava | Beating through
Her unleashing heart

In a zap | She was on me | Words firing out
Machine-gun style | Pelting me| Every angle | Jabbing at
Uncovered emotions | My face turning | Significantly violet red
From the adjectives | Hurled into | The surrounding space
Between our bodies

This was the exact moment | I knew
I loved this woman
Her honesty | Her truth | Her fire | Burning me
Like never before | Inflaming my | Forest of desire

She left that night | The night of the desert wind
Leaving with | The slamming of the door
A middle finger shooting up | Towards the heavens
Her venom | Spewing words | I could no longer
Even understand | As the driveway dirt | Lost itself
In the bitter wind | I smiled | Deep joy | Flooding my spirit
Understanding so deeply | She would return
Unable to escape
The fiery passions
So clearly stoked
Within the raging fire
Our love

"Lady in Red Shoes,"
Port Ceresio, Italy

Lightning Kiss

Her smile

Pearlescent whites | Lips lustrous and nude

Drawing the focus | Of everything within its view

A spinning vortex | Drawing fire and desire

Unknowing individuals | Blindly obedient

Hungry eyes guiding the way

Lightning kissing the ground | Causing a burn

Aching to the lonely core | Providing glowing

Atomic energy | Filtering through the stagnant air

Lungs breathing in supercharged energy

Allowing the violent warm surge

Pounding through a willing heart

Gaining momentum

My brain

Dancing in the surge

The Great Spirit

A long time ago
The Great Spirit | Was there | Was everything
Within everything

Knowing humanity could not understand | What was, was
A decision was made | To split into two
Yin and yang   Masculine and feminine
Light and Dark   Sun and Moon
One not better than the other | Equally magnificent
Equally alive | Equally reflecting |The Spirits essence

The feminine
Hurled high into the sky | Discovered in the moon's dark rays
Magically placed | Within this earth | Called Mother Nature |
Sent us alive, growing | Sensual and mysterious
Green, purple, yellow | Gold and red | Maroon, blue and pink
Colors reflecting | Passion in compassion | Intimacy
The desire to embrace | A desire to be connected intimately
Inviting humanity | To enter into Her | To be swallowed by Her
To be found within Her bosom

Great Spirit
Hurled in the sky | The sun | Masculine and strong
Vibrant and alive | Guiding throughout the lighted day
Being willing | Forging ahead | Day after day
As the light | The measure | North and south | East and west |

Strong and vibrant | Intense at times | Reliable and safe
Trusting and protective

The Heavens
Hurled into place | When looking up
The great Spirit could be seen | The essence of that Spirit
In every star | Every solar system | Every inch of it

It's all there | To fully embrace
It's all there | To fully accept

If we see it | We have no choice
But to live it
I believe it | I can feel it | Embracing it | As Truth

The Way

Trevor Hall's song "Green Mountain State" played as I wrote this piece.

There is a Way
    One that offers
        Joy, peace, and Love
It blows | In the growing green Aspen leaves
Following these same | Browning leaves
Floating through
    The crisp air
        As they miraculously feed
           The ground below
This Way
Lightens the load | Allowing for fresh lungs | Expanding into
Taking in the newness | Light-hearted laughter
Recognizing the opportunity | Found within pain
Ongoing struggle
This Way
Allowing space | For our infant souls | Born on a wheel
Rolling west | Towards the expanding skyline
Embracing the now | Knowing the Great Spirit
Offers the Way | Deliciously sucking it fully in

"Leading West," Stanley Lake, Westminster, Colorado

Beauty Bearers

We are beauty bearers
Of the Great Spirit | Believing everyone
Has inward beauty | We're all born | With, and within
This beauty | A Light | Meant to shine

Unfortunately for a lot of us | That beauty was hidden
Put down | Beat down | Used for artificial gain
Prostituted and lied too | Words were formed

Of not being enough
 Not being pretty enough
 Handsome enough
 Thin enough
 Athletic enough
Putting down | Of our being | Universal Love

The Great Spirit | Lives for beauty | Flourishing with beauty
Look in a mirror | Your reflection back | Shines a beauty
Living within | Look deeply | See and believe
That reflective beauty
Is YOU

A SUNFLOWER SHE IS

blown in the wind
born into unforgiving soil | forced to grow
little food | littler water | surviving on the extremes
overexposure to
the darkness | Underexposed of the light
somehow, she grew | strengthening with each breath
moving forward | protecting | a fragile heart | kindness
being her | guiding light | North Star | within the dark night
her spirit
learning to thrive | serving others
with every healing stroke | of the Universe's brush
humbly allowing | her gentle seeds | to be sown
into the weary | like a rancher | she calls her stallions
her growing tribe | to experience connecting | diving into
the healing waters | of the community pool
a marvel she is
awakening and sensuous | delightful and brave
future breaths untapped | moving towards | the gentle horizon

"Light in Darkness," Westminster, Colorado

Seeds

A gifting | The Mothers gentle touch
Blown passionately | In the wind
Swirling gifts | Settling in the dirt

Seeds...

A kiss | Universal Love | Passing gently
From one to another | The tiniest of giving
Often creating | The greatest impact

Seeds...

Rooting within | Hardened rock
Fertile soil | Not mattering
To the giver | Shared lovingly

Seeds...

Making the universe whole | Allowing life
To continue | Enabling love
To fully blossom | Continuing the giving cycle

Seeds...

Exploding into | Onto our desperate
Lonely, cynical world | Inviting new growth
Expanding the reach | Of Loves gentle embrace

PART 3

HEALING

INTRODUCTION

T his part is titled Healing because I was no longer teetering on the edge of healing, I was starting to bathe within its beauty. The time period was from November 2020 through October 2021. Moments of joy cause me to smile and celebrate unlike any other moment in my life. These moments allow me to enter back into my trauma to allow a deep cleansing unlike any other time before it.

During this time the words Dancing DNA showed up. I was writing about an experience with my good friend Mark Whitney at a Metallica concert in Denver. I was referring to music and its unique ability to serve as a bridge connecting us to emotions and deep-seated places that nothing else seems to be able to bring out. It was in this season that I experienced the symphony for the first time. I started listening to jazz, and I heard my first live opera. All these new "firsts" in my life paved the way for new growth as they watered the seeds of the past couple years of my writing.

Joy and Grief: Alive and Risking

Living

At the intersection | Joy and grief
Joyfully celebrating | A season | Loving another
Fully integrating | Their energy into mine

Loving

Being loved | Celebrating | Being celebrated
Basking in the joy | And light | Found in two
Flaming seeds | Found within | Lover's embrace

Emotions

Sharing the stage | With thick grief
A grief | Blinding to | My sight
Causing internal bleeding | With my soul
Needing a transfusion | Waking to a wall
Heaviness | Greeting me | A teeth stained smile
Gripping me | As I slip | Into the covers at night
Every day | That passes | I step | I survive

Tenacity

I was born into | Flashes profusely | Before my eyes
I adapt | And awaken more | To the beauty
Surrounding me | Living within me
Love is my guide | Her precious energy | Oozing from within

Learning

I'm learning | To fully trust | My emotions
Their *tells* | Leading me | Where I need to be
I'm learning | To fully hope | To speak | To the universe
The mighty Guide | About a future | A desire
I live | With kindness | Sharing truth | Not as a weapon
Desiring to draw out | The best in another

Breathing

I breathe | In intimacy | Desiring it more | With every
Sunrise that awaits | This purpose | Slowly removing
The extreme sadness | Accompanying the grief
That is present | Like a fog | I know | I believe
That life only stops | If I choose | To allow it to do so
Therefore, I am | Alive and risking
The breath | Coming with | This glorious day

"Lake Trail," Black Lake, Rocky Mountain National Park

Why So Sad?

Awakening to
A wall
Grief
Slipping into bed
Hugging me
Like a lover
Tightly spooning
Sadness
A state of being
Once controlling
A massive part
Of my daily energy

Diligently working | Not wanting
It's depressing clutches | On me again
Suffering through | A tremendous loss
A ripping heart | Yearning to feel one
So much a part | Of my daily life
My thoughts | Words alive
For many months Trying to wade through
The murky waters | Of being thankful
For the season | Of love and laughter
While honoring | The space
Of an unfolding tragedy within

For me | Everyday holds | The process of appreciating

The gift | I was given | From the universe
While allowing | Tears to flow | I no longer
Live with walls | Allowing myself | To live
To breath | To exist | In a yurt | Slowly removing
The doors | And barriers | Keeping me
From fully experiencing my life | Yet lived
I hike | The Colorado trails | With thankfulness
For one | So lovely | And the time | Spent together
I watch | The sunrise | Exploding every day
Thankfully accepting | The gift | Grief and sadness
Are bestowing | Upon me

"Shadow Play,"Boulder Bandshell, Boulder, Colorado

Untethered Me

Laying quietly | The yoga mat | Hugging my body
Breathing at a minimum | Fully in the moment | This moment
The serenity | Of this sacred place
The voice of one | Lovely and skilled

An image | Little Ricky | Slowly moving
No longer in a fog | Bringing pain | With it
Welcoming him | Embracing him | Allowing his presence
His laugh | To freely ring | Enveloping me
Echoing within

I'm him | Running as little Ricky | Breaking free
From a mother's clutch | Strong and cold | Touching
Alaskan dirt | Rubbing its grittiness onto | Glowing skin
Laughing eyes | Dancing within | A vibrant blue sky

I am | I am Rick | I am Rick Love
I am Rick Love Ellsmore
I am Rick, Ricky, Love Ellsmore
I am bold | I am free | I am
What I've always dreamed of being
Untethered
ME

"Little Ricky," Taken day after my mom's death in Indiana, Pennsylvania

ON FIRE

The rhythm | Calling me inward
While mysteriously | Drawing me outward
Movement mixing | With the sound | Of her voice
Smooth and alive | Words spoken | The sound of my voice
Alive and awake | Strong and bold | Flames flowing | Up from
Mother Earth | Grounded and pure | Confiscating my essence
Becoming fire | Flames burning | Standing up
Heat rushing into | All my limbs
Enveloping me | In sweet bliss
Not wanting | To stop the beauty
Of the blaze | Oranges and reds | White hot heat
Dancing in my calm | Elevating essence | Consuming me
Into the now | Burn baby burn | Seer me | With your
Eternal fire

Draw me | Into you
Into this | Magnificent dance

The Warrior's Edge

The Kriya beginning | A rhythmic movement
Automatically kicking in

My inner fire igniting | The pilot light being lit
Breath work | Using both nostrils | Pumping my heart
Into fluid action | Specific motions

Opening up the roots | Anticipating what is to come
Time flows | My voice inflamed
Drawn to the surface | Warming up | On a cold fall night
Stepping into | A warrior's pose
One Kriya | Two Kriya | Three Kriya deep
Words flying | Holding in the air | From her strong voice

The sacred feminine is smooth fluid motion
The sacred masculine movements are with specific purpose
Own your movement, allow your voice to be heard

Letting go | My voice echoing | Off the floor
Bouncing from the walls | Sounding like thunder
Shaking the air | Fully capturing
Allowing the energy | Of this moment | Igniting
The fire within | Becoming the lion | Feeling its breath
Burn through my lungs | My tongue extended
As the rhythmic sound | Of my inner voice

Engages the roar | Of 1000 sparks | Tears welling up
Slowly flowing | As I feel | The inner Guide
Pouring warmth | Through all | Of my being
Liquid love | Seeping into | All of the exposed
Hidden gaps within

A shift moving in | The form of a dance | Moving back
From the warrior's edge | The rhythmic touch
Of the didgeridoo | Piercing my voice | Dancing movement
Flowing in | The music | Causing hands and hips
To engage | Letting go | Eyes no longer
Fiercely open | Dancing with | My Venus moon
Allowing the flow | Of her magnificent energy
Carrying me | Back into the rhythm | Of the Yin

Sitting on | My thick blue mat | Fully understanding
The magnitude | Of the experience | I had just experienced
Like the movement | Of the Kriya | My present | My future
Exposed and engaged

"Overlooking the Edge," Loveland Pass, Colorado

Liquid Love

I was tired | Dead tired
I needed | A shot of yoga
The class | Smooth and tough
Right on point | calling us
To the edge | My body reacting
By allowing it to | Be pushed
Finishing up | We went | Into our savasana | I felt something
Deeper moving in | Not needing to do anything | But allow
Tears slowly forming
I found myself | Moving toward a cliff
Overlooking a vast ocean | Moving closer
The present edge | Ignoring my fear
Heights alive | No desire to jump
The sea | Alive and blue
It's sensuous sounds
Calling me inward
I hear her voice
Active and soft
Inviting me
To the water's edge
Enticing me | To look deeply
Deeply into Her eyes | Staring profoundly
Seeing myself | Within her liquid love
Enveloping my being | Tears starting to gush|
The wave of her beauty | Splashing through

My attuned essence | Slowly being called
Back to the awake | Moment upon moment
Awakening passion
Streaming from Her | Into me
Gasping for breath
I mouth | I don't have the words
But I will write them
This moment | Feeling my fluid self
Unlike before
Knowing the significance
Of this day | November 7, 2020
It's remarkable discovery
Enrapturing Love | In Love
With Love | Loving the life | I've been gifted

"Holding Venus," San Juan, Puerto Rico

Becoming Love

I can actually | Feel love
Not an emotion
It's in the air | It's in everyone
Often hidden | Not to me
I see
I feel
I sense
Because I am | Love
Put on earth | To walk beside
The broken
The beaten
Those who can't see | Desiring to see | To be known
Love
Like a warm | Summer breeze | Has arrived
Encompassing all
I am | Becoming all | I do | She's the very fabric
From which I was sewn
We all are sewn

HO'OPONOPONO

I'm sorry | Please forgive me | Thank you | I love you

Whispered from | My mouth | To myself
The sweat | Still fresh | On my body
Our guide | Eloquently leading | Us through
The yoga practice | For the day

Movements | Graceful and silky
Specifically designed
Of body
Of mind
Of spirit
Calling me deeper | Into myself
These precious words
Sorry
Forgive
Thank you
Love
Hanging in the air | Like stars | On a crystal-clear night
Boring deep | Within my soul | Causing a physical reaction
Goosebumps | Alligator tears | Slowly starting
Spreading over | My entire being | Slowly dripping down
My chin | Onto my chest
Warm tears
Tears from | A lifetime of struggling and pain

Pools of love | Calling me back | To my first love | Me
Inviting me
To forgive
Accept
I'm sorry
Words to myself | Please forgive me | Words to myself
Thank you | Words to myself | I love you | Words to myself
Honoring words | Echoing words | From an ancient practice
Calling upon | Ancestors and Spirit | Directing my now
Giving meaning
To my coming joy

Dancing DNA

This was the first time this phrase entered my vocabulary.

The music begins | A slow rise
   The sea of sound | Slowly rolling in
      My senses fluidly | Coming alive
        The drums | Beating to my heart
      The power cords | Of the electric guitar
    Bringing forth | An eruption of emotion
  The bass bringing bone-crushing
Internal intersecting | Then the voice
Kicks in | The perfect pitch
  Matching the intensity | Of the perfectly timed beat
    My DNA changing | Becoming more
      More of | What I'm meant to be
        Awakening the deepening me | Inviting more of me
      To the surface
    My body | Automatically moving
  The music's power | Drawing out
My dancing DNA
  Emotions surging | To the surface
    The intersection points | Changing me
      Never to be the same | From the music
      Blasting through my speakers
      My mind | Cataloging this moment
    One I will | Remind myself of

Many times | Going back | Basking in
The beauty experienced | In that one
  Perfect moment
    Music causing | My dancing DNA
  To come alive | Orgasmic experiencing
Never to be | Exactly the same

"Dancing Friends," my best friend, Mark Whitney,
at Metallica in Denver, Colorado

The Edge

I felt the blade | Digging deep into
Exposed raw flesh | Dragging me towards

The Edge

Not wanting these emotions | Their darkness present
My fear binding | Then the gush
Words, tears, snot | Flowing into the chasm
Felt within | A damn breaking
Allowing for | Small fresh breaths of air

A Gift

Sharing with | A dear friend
No allowing shame | Or wanting fear
To reign on the throne | Entering yoga
My daily trip to Ceremony | Finding a welcoming
In the three present souls | Each unique and shining
Lights of kindness | Feeling and smelling of home
My spirit raging against| The breathing and stretching
Being offered to me | A gift wrapped in prickly paper
The movement slowly eroding | My hesitation and boundness
Like a mudslide | After a torrential rainstorm
My emotions starting | To cave and slide
Towards center | Back to my roots

SA-TA-NA-MA
Two yoga exercises | Bringing me closer
Drawing out | The binding poison
The first | A song we sang
Using our fingers | Touching each one
The sensation | Mixing with the words
Wrapped within | The music
Causing an inner gush | Awakening my desire
SA-TA-NA-MA
Echoing over and over | From my voice
From the collective | Of four participants
Sa... *birth, beginning*
Ta... *Life, existence*
Na... *Death, transformation*
Ma... *rebirth, regeneration*
(Taken from Yogapedia)
Awe flooding my system | Fusing fire and water
Into a shining experience
Reflecting the way home

The Edge

The other | Was a stretching
"Figure Four" was what she called it
My thighs crying out | The longer holding
This specific pose | Not inching
Sprinting towards the knife's edge | My body wanting to
Escape the boundary | At all costs
To bail out of the pain | Choosing a different way
Spirit reminding me | Allow the edge to be

Choosing the pain | Moving towards
The edge collapsing | From being a blade
Becoming a cliff's perch | Standing looking out

Beauty

The sea and Her | Luxurious beauty
Inviting me to rest | The edge of pain
Still having a presence | No longer the center
A knowing | I was meant for | This adventure
Found at this edge
The Edge, The Spirit | The Fire, The All
Calling me | Wooing me | HOME

Beauty so Deep

Beauty so deep
Who could sleep

Love comes down
Through the town

With a jolly laugh
Coming forth on behalf

Each and every soul
Awaiting more than coal

Loves sweet kiss
Causing a stir of eternal bliss

"Xmas Beauty," Downtown Parker, Colorado

BORN TO
WONDER

We were | Born to wonder
A Divine curiosity | Straining through
Open veins | Desirous of | The Light
Aging slowly eroding | Joy's questioning
Life besting us | Causing Spirit
Hunkering down | Packed tightly
Into a cocooned heart Until one
Blessed moment | Reborning day
Glorious moments | Bubbling to
The dry surface
The dessert
Receiving the downpour
Inviting the green | The color
The refreshing beauty | To blossom
Colors anew | Familiar in
A deja vu echo | Bringing out
Orange and purple | Blue's streaming
Interjecting giggling warmth
Born to run | We are
Vagabonds on | This spinning sphere
No longer living flat | Joining together
Exploding anew | The joining
Have joined | Swirling in
The Mother's lovely embrace

"Awakening Wonder," Camelback Mountain,
Phoenix, Arizona

Reuniting Ancient Halls

She is | No ball and chain
She is freedom's kiss
She loves | By releasing | By trusting
By believing
My heart is good
My heart is full
My heart is kind
My heart longs
My heart desires
My heart lusts
After more of her | Deeper within
Welcoming rhythm | Calling us home
Calling her | To the surface
Allowing him | To the surface
Reuniting ancient halls | Filled with energy
Allowing for | The gods of Love | Consuming old wounds
Inviting fresh movement | Kiss upon kiss
Kindness upon kindness | Love upon love
We are home

"Castle Hall,"Wawel Royal Castle, Krakow, Poland

Intersection

Past and future | Connecting in the present
The weight of it | Causing a heaviness
Boa constrictor-like emotion

Circling

There truly is | A circle to life
Intersecting point | When old | Crashes into the new
I'm good, really good | At putting my full weight
Behind something | Going all in | Selling out
Pushing balance | Beyond its capability | Holding
But yet | I'm not so good | At sitting within
Processing through | The grief | The pain
The trauma | The things that can't be rushed
Pushed through | Especially the ones
That won't go away | Those old wounds | Old voices
I'm discovering | They come back up | Most often
More loudly | Clanging like kitchen dishes
In the early morning

Honoring

Do I give them the attention they need?
The focus they deserve?
Do I honor them?
Or do I move on?

Band-aiding them | Hoping they will
Heal themselves
I'm in a season of honesty | Brutal rawness
I've been wrestled | To the ground
Demanding to be heard | Liquifying my resistance
In this moment | I'm learning
To not give up | Rather, to give in
Learning a deeper level | Of trusting myself
Which in turn | Allowing love
The kindness | The strength
That is discovered | On the other side

"Into," Westminster, Colorado

Build It

If you build it | He will come
I've seen the movie | *Field of Dreams*
For over 20 years | Every few years | Allowing myself
To enter back into | The sacred ground | Of this classic movie

Magic

There is magic to it | As the years have gone by | I always
Envisioned it being | About my father | A siren's call
To a relationship | I never got to experience
I've thought this | Until I watched it
This last time | I'm watching it now
As I take this in

Building

If you build it | He will come
This statement | Means much more
At this important moment | In some ways
The most important moment | In my life
If I build it | I BUILD IT | Build my home | Build trust
Within myself | A new knowing | That until I'm happy
There truly is no one | Who can make me happy

Trusting

Until I fully trust myself | I can never | Fully trust another
He will come | The real me | The content me | The me
That's built upon | A security found | Within me
Built upon an understanding | That if the Divine
Lives within me | Within us | Then I | Then we
Are of the Divine | The universe | True Love
Therefore, everything | I need | Is already living
Within

Letting Go

So I'm working | No I'm finally loosening my grip
Letting go | Finally understanding | If I build it
If I plow under the corn | The corn | Being the old way
Of doing things
If I trust | A trust built upon | Believing in myself
Allowing the seasons to flow
Then he will come
The HE | Found in me
The one | I've searched my life for
HE
WILL
COME

her

|———————|

her *touch*
a feather on my skin
her *voice* a whisper
reverberating echoes
afloat in my mind
her *kiss*
expanding a withered heart
to love again

"Silky Goosebumps," NCAR Mesa Trail, Boulder, Colorado

It's Beauty

The words | Flooding my senses
Tears streaming down | It's BEAUTY
I had some friends | Ask me about my tats
The question
With a body covered in words
What is the most important word
On your body?
I immediately | Without hesitation
Went to
BEAUTY
On my left inner bicep
Kind of surprised myself | Stunned me actually
There is a seed | One I'm understanding
Unlike the comprehension | I've had for anything
Before this moment
I, Rick Ellsmore
Am about BEAUTY
I see it | I smell it | I understand it
I share it | I find it
In most any settings | I point it out | I pull it out
Separating | Wheat from the chaff
Why do I do this?
How do I do this?
There is a small voice | Growing in substance
Helping me to understand | It's because of

A life spent | Searching for the Light
That I now can understand BEAUTY
In understanding Beauty
I can comprehend most anything
There are so many places | To go with BEAUTY
The ultimate BEAUTY | Is the BEAUTY
That resides inside
If I can somehow | Come to terms
With my BEAUTY
Then I can allow others | To find their shine
The beauty that desires | To enrapture them
I'm reminded | That we are created
In the image
Of the Divine
The ultimate BEAUTY
A Universal BEAUTY
Undefined | A shine so bright

"You Are Beautiful," Boulder, Colorado

Back to Extremes

2021 - Taking life to the extreme

Grinding

I tried living without sleep – 15 hours in 5 days
Yoga | Work
Hiking | Art
Pain | Pushing me along
Driving me | Toward an edge
I barely made it back
The opposite | Slowing life to a crawl
Somedays | Yes, some whole days
Counting the minutes | Grinding through days
Weeks | Even a month

Extremely Slowly

Living life at a snail's pace | Enduring the darkness
The exact opposite | Of the light
Felt not so long ago | Balancing the line
The meeting of the yin | With the yang
Living in | The very moment | They meet
Wu Wei
Serving as | Breadcrumbs
Toward an unknown present
Unexperienced and unlived | Silent awaiting
My arrival

Why Do I Write?

Why do I write?
A question pondered
Like never before
For me? | For others?
To be liked? | Or admired?
Similar to | An old rusty
Muscle car | Resting on
A vacant field | I have Stripped
this one back
Layer by layer
Rust piling | At my feet
The luster | Clearly gone
In walking away
From the daily act
Discovering | The gold
The heart | The meaning
write | For me
Writing to explore
To uncover
To experience
The Divine | The me
Found only
In uncovered words
Words I love

No, words I adore Stabilizers
Shoring up Areas wanting
To sink
There is brutal-ness
To the process
Uncovering a deep
Long-held need
To be seen
Using words
To further convince
I am worthy | Of love
Of admiration
This old need
Melting away | Butter
On a hot pancake
The reasoning behind
These choices
No longer | Needing
To be fed
I'm becoming | Me Living
Within fresh dew
Of the luxurious
New dawn
Beautifully laid out
In front of me

I

"Pondering," Julius Breckling Riverfront Park, Little Rock, Arkansas

PART 4

REBIRTH

INTRODUCTION

Ah, the word *rebirth*. I love this and the beauty found in any kind of birthing. My Celtic roots run deep as I am ultra-aware of the seasons and the spiritual affect they have on me and how I witness and experience nature around me. It was during this time, November 2021 through January 2023, that I reentered the dating scene after an eighteen-month period of celibacy to continue my process of healing.

During this time, my writing took on a different tone. This sacred evolving opened up areas of myself that I never even knew existed. The reality that everything is poetry, or poetic, has finally sunk in. Every detail of every one of our days has a poetic nature to it. It was during this time that I reoriented my thinking about relationships—both with good friends and with a lover. I began to understand the beauty found within each moment experienced together, allowing myself to surrender into the higher gift, or higher love, that was there for me. This gift, intertwining with truth, served as a siren's call as I reoriented my life and found the peace and contentment I so desired.

Within this blossoming love I also discover the yin and yang found in the process of living. The deepening reality that pain and pleasure are so significantly connected. Stepping deep into the balance that my desire to skip, or only go part way into the pain, was enough. I now know this to not be true. There is no way to avoid the pain and skip right to the good stuff. The great news is that we *can* experience the good stuff! The dancing part. The moving within the flow of this moment in our lives. And further, we will be okay. On the other side of pain is joy.

Radiant

Grosse Ausstrahlung
In German | Meaning *radiance* | Oh, what a majestic word

What comes to mind?

I think of the Rocky Mountains | Driving west on Route 36
Deeper into Boulder | Breathless strength | Awaiting me

I think of Naomi | My four-month-old niece
Laughs and giggles | Flowing like magic

I think of an image | A lady's fiery blue eyes
Translucent snowflakes | Fluttering through my brain

Majestic moments | Magic to the soul | Beauty personified
The essence | Of being alive

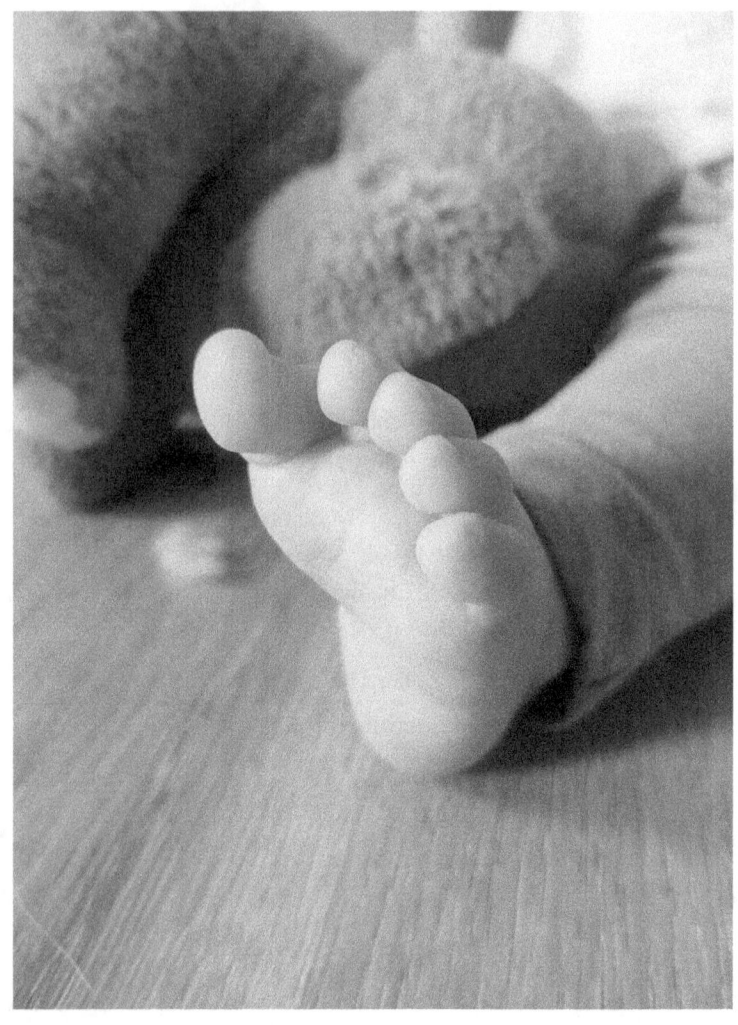

Tiny Toes," My great niece, Naomi's toes, Ashburn, Virginia

Dance Yourself Clean

I stood outside | Getting some air
A rare intermission | At a concert
A dude standing there | Belting out
DANCE YOURSELF CLEAN!
My appetite for words | Well fed
Especially in the full body expression
He shared them in

Words describing | An incredible evening | The energy
Surrounding it | Beautiful and pure | No pretension or ego
Being fully present | A pure running stream
Joy and fun
What could he have meant?
DANCING | Moving in selfish pleasure
Or entertaining others
YOURSELF | The person we see in the mirror | That special
person | Unearthed often when alone
CLEAN | Freeing ourselves from staining or being dirty

I loved these words this dude shared
Where do we go to remove the grime Constantly building up?
You know | The greasy skin feeling
Coming from the toxins | Of modern living
Media
Relationship drama
Pain and shame
Fear and anxiety
The negative barnacles | Clinging desperately to our skin

While dancing the night away | Watching the loveliest
Of female creatures | I got a taste of heaven
Allowing the incredible sound | Visual stimulation
To wash over me

Walking out of Mission Ballroom | With my adorable
Concert buddy | She explained | Concerts and dancing
Are her church | A place to be alive | Letting go | Connecting
With a Source | The Source
A moment in time | One never forgotten | Capturing stardust
And worship
Permanent glitter
Still shimmying
On my translucent skin

"Dancing Clean," Levitt Pavilion, Denver, Colorado

-simple kiss-

have you ever thought
how much kissing
is taken for granted
not meaning | a kiss on the cheek
i mean a passionate | wet, soul shuddering
kiss
on the lips
is a simple kiss, so simple?
the zap | the instant the energy is transferred
from one to another | a gateway drug | to deeper connecting
something that | typically pulling us closer
to another | or farther away
depending on the | butterflies showing up
in our stomachs | or maybe the zap
coming from something so simple | as another's tongue
whether it's kissing tag | as a child
or someone | you've been married to for years
every single kiss | is a decedent
a reminder of Universal LOVE
a connection point
a moment
moving us from ourselves | into the world | of another
where the water meets the land
the stars settle in the sky

the eyes twinkle connecting to another
the edge of the extravagant
wouldn't that make this act | One of holiness
a Divine act of sharing
something to celebrate | not to be taken for granted
i'm probably thinking of it more
because it's been a while
but like all things in life | fate seems to come calling

TRAGICAL ROMANCE

What draws
Us back wanting
Time and time again
Pulling us towards heartbreaking story
To the tragedy often discovered in romance
Is it the adventure filled buildup giving us hope
Could it be the succulent moment when lovers meld together
I believe it to be the connection, magic dust, settling in
Two lost souls becoming found with another
The moments together seemingly making
All of the pain and sorrow disappear
I've experienced my tragical
It has left me wanting
Desiring a romance
That will last
Beyond
Tragic
Into
The
Now

"Heart Magic," Elk Meadows Park, Evergreen, Colorado

Amazing You

You are amazing
Remember that | A-m-a-z-i-n-g
Why is it so difficult to remember this very thing?
Why is forgetting so easy to do?
Why are the negatives sitting so close to the top of our garden?
The work | Of getting to the healthy
Having to dig so much deeper
Rotten veggies | Negative self-talk
Self-hatred | Rearing ugly heads
Spoiling what is to be | The ripeness
The freshness | Arriving within self-love
Self-appreciation
What does it look like to root out?
Digging deep | Remove the poison found within
What does it look like to allow? | The ripe
The good | The rich
The echoes | From heaven | Universe Love
Meant for each of us | Blossoming within

Comfort and Joy

May *comfort* find you
In the sweet taste | Of dark chocolate | On your tongue

May *luxury* envelope you
In the surrounding texture | Of the softest blanket
Upon your skin

May holiday *warmth*
Encase all your senses

May joy's *delight*
Ooze into | All areas of your body | Reaching and filling
Your expanding heart
And LOVE'S gentle kiss

"Ornament Beauty," Westminster, Colorado

Knick-Knacks

This is how the conversation went:

"I also like to see people's knick-knacks"

"Oh wait, that sounds a bit frisky"

"That's super cute frisky"

"Can I see your knick-knacks sometime?"

"We will have to see won't we

It's fun to think about... Showing you my knick-knacks

But you know, one day at a time"

"Oh, but I do like to touch knick-knacks

Just an FYI, I'm very tactile that way"

"You like to touch Knick-knacks? (-: "

"I'm going to go out on a limb here

But I bet you have delightful knick-knacks"

"Well, my kick-knacks like to be admired! Hahaha"

"Delightful indeed

Well, I hope to get to admire them!"

Ahh that energy | Laughter freely flowing

Floating luxuriously in the air | Surrounding words

Written out | Crafted from | Two minds ablaze

Flirting being | A love language | Rarely spoken

Something else in common

Our conversation | Jumping to other things

Fun things | Deep things | Unearthing a wealth

A gold mine | Of potential conversations
To be had

Here is
To hoping
They are had!

"Chess Mate," Keep Tryst Manor, Knoxville, Maryland

THE ANSWER?

⊢————⊣

*Bruce Springsteen's "War" and Bob Dylan's "Union Sundown" played
when I wrote this poem.*

Is violence the answer?
What about war?
What the hell is it for?

As a young man | I grew up with the words…
Violence is never the answer
Hollow words | Shared from
A place of privilege | Ones overflowing
With hypocrisy

Living in a house | A community
Celebrating the loss of JFK & MLK
Claiming Christianity | Was about love
Yet, outwardly celebrating
As bombs destroyed abortion clinics
Hopefully killing the doctors committing crimes

Our history | Littered with war
The blood of millions | Spilling upon our country
Our world
And for what?

Land?
Property?
So called freedom?
Power?

We woke up to war
Abhorrently playing out | Videos live streaming
On billions of screens
I'm taken | By the extreme contrast
Sitting last week | The lovely notes
Of the Denver Symphony | Melding so gorgeously
With the prophetic words | Of Bob Dylan
His desire for peace | Filling the night
With compassion | Love's tender embrace
His brilliant song, Union Sundown
Saying what needs | To be said

It's become pretty simple | For me | Fuck war!
And it's death, destruction, and pain
The innocent paying
For the rapacious bloodlust
Of our so-called world leaders

The Sea

The sea
    She is so sexy
Indeed
    Movement galore
A lovely lady
    Fluid
        Coming and going
          Yet always present
            Having a hard edge
            Falling from
            The sky
The water's edge   Breaking bones powerful
        But yet
To the touch
M e l t i n g in your fingers
Bringing instant life   With Her essence
She is | Sensuous mystery | Alluring senses alive

Caught in a Moment

Stunned to silence
Stunning my emotions
A deer captured by the Light | Stealing my breath
Silently moving my essence | The tiniest of fibers | Bubbling
One at a time | All going silent | Only to explode
In my aroused mind
She is
Caught in a moment
The eye of the artist | Capturing her essence
The sheer beauty | Of her curves | Feminine creases
Causing the eye | To roam and explore | Freedom's delight
Shimmering down | A back | So voluptuously created
Strength in hands | Clearly seen | The Designer's touches
Gorgeously illustrating | Her contouring toes

She is
Caught in the moment
Captured forever
Causing a twinkle to all that are blessed
To bask within
Her divine beauty

Ocean Blue

I'm at peace | Calm and warm
The Flow of blue | A streak of joy
Pulsating lovingly
Through my willing vessel
I walked the beach | Endlessly searching
Shell after shell | Only leaving me
Emptier with | Each lonely touch
The sea | She whispered | Slowly softly
Stop looking | She is coming | My feet
Gently traversing| The warm sand
A new tide | Rolling in
Pulsating warmth | Looking down
I saw it | A heart
Meant just for me | As it slid
Perfectly fitting my hand
Finding its way | To my heart
Within the Rush | Came one
Lovely and blue | Emanating Love
Every pore | Surrounding me
With brilliant silver light
She has found me
In me
Finding Her

"North Sea Beauty," The Hague, Netherlands

LIFETIMES
OF LOVE

The smoke
Wafting to the sky
The smoke hole
In the tipi
Giving a glimpse
Of the stars above
Twinkling in delight
At the magic
Being shared
Under these skins
The warmth of the brown fur
Rubbing gently | Upon exposed dark skin

Her breath | Fresh from berries and garden
Sharing delight   She smells
Earth and Wind A representative
Of the Holy One   The Mother

A celebration   The Mother's delight
The greatest gift | Given to the Earth | Her presence
Causing Every Living Creature   To Take Notice
To Perk Up   To Taste

Glimpsing Beauty	She Brings Joy
A Joy Flowing	Like A Fresh
Colorado Streams	Blossoming Spring
Blowing From Her Being	Drawing Me Back
Into Her Bosom	One Known
For Generations	Lifetimes Ago

Bringing forth a trust | A bubbling joy | Never experienced

A child running loose | Laughing within
 Swinging from
Father Oak
From brother Aspen | From sister Pine
A moment in time
Hoping and desiring
Anticipating delight
Felt deeper | With each | Passing moment

Lives intertwined | Truth and magic
The elixir | Causing delight
To dance magnificently | Upon the drifting sands
Of the Universe

She is Fire
She is Wind
She was found
Within the dance
Dancing Fire Wind
I worship with you

"Angel Wings," San Juan, Puerto Rico

All... Is Poetry

I am... Poetry
We are... Poetry
Life is... Poetry
Feminine is... Poetry
Masculine is... Poetry
The Moon is... Poetry
The Sun is... Poetry
The Universe is... Poetry
Further...
Sex is... Poetry
Sexual intimacy is... Poetry
Fingers are... Poetry
Touch is... Poetry
Hugs are... Poetry
Love is.. Poetry

We Scream; I Scream

We scream | I scream
For ice cream
Chocolate dripping | A slow ride
Down the side | Causing a glide
Making me | Want to abide
Moving to a groove | One that's got me
On the move | Wanting to remove
Not needing | To prove
The excitement and joy
This little toy | Brings to this boy
Ice cream | Causing a stir
No longer a blur
Not needing | A savior
Rather a playmate | To inflate
My growing interstate
Moving and grooving joy
Ice Cream screaming | Us dripping
Dancing | Sugar | Licking lips | Playing

Body Hatred

I grew up chubby
One of the most prevalent facts | Remembering of my childhood

Memories

Before 15
Body hatred | Body shaming
A debilitating shadow
    Pee Wee
    Fat boy
    Slow footed
    Uncoordinated dough boy
Words echoing | Hollowing memories
Bouncing off | My lonely room walls
So much attention | Placed on looks
Outer shell

My family | Well, the parents who raised me
Playing along | With the jokes
My father | Often the ringleader
Inventing "nicknames" | Slicing and cutting
From Gunsmoke | From his upbringing
To noisy | To messy | Mistake prone
Negativity serving | As the bad breath

Breathing fire | Upon my young soul
Wounds never healing | Before another
Sliced into another part | Of my soft body

Destroying

Early on | I sensed his fear | His hatred
For his own | Sinful flesh | Words hurling
Wolf's breath | Blowing down | His own house
Taking with it | The flesh | Surrounding and protecting
The shell around | His son's tender heart

Most days | Wanting to mutilate this body
Dreaming of cutting off fat | Envying most
Everyone I saw
A battle | I have waged | My entire life

New Day

Today is a new day | One filling | With life-giving hope
Eleanor Roosevelt's affirming words
"Do one thing every day that scares you"
Serving as a reminder
The fat boy | Has gone | Replaced with a body
I have always desired | One I'm thankful for
Every single day | Even with the abs | I've always desired
Body crafted by hard work | And nature
I have to own | This body | To love it
To hug it | To embrace it
In its flaws | And beauty

Fear

Today 7.9.22 | Is one of those days
No longer allowing my fear | Of being seen
To stop me | No longer hiding | Welcoming the fear
Allowing it | To be heard | Inviting it | To join me
As I launch
Where?
At the Denver Tattoo Convention
Where my tattoos | Beautifully crafted
By Dree | Will be on display
An inner thigh | An Orca piece
The one | Being voted upon | The Ink Masters | Eyeing my
Exposed skin | Along with | All the others
Tattooed brothers | And sisters | At the convention

I step into fear | Allowing my beauty | To be seen
Through my exposing words | With skin made anew
Art and gifted Love

"Ricky," My sixth-grade picture

WANT-NEED-
DESERVE

|———————|

This journey | Taking me deeper
Tumbling down | The rabbit hole
Closer to the center | My center
The centering | Of my personhood
Discovering peace | That well
Only found within | This journey
The past few months | Bringing clarity
Rich understanding | More of myself
Being found | The holding | Of the key
In my hands

What do I want and desire?
Important question
To not be alone | I've spent so much of my life alone
Time with a lover | Someone I can | Freely give to
Someone who | Can accept | My gifts

What do I need?
Very important | To understand this
Communication | In all forms
Honesty | Kind and caring soul | Healthy boundaries
Strong self-evaluator | Playfulness | Someone who listens

What do I deserve?
I deserve it all | Fairly simple | To me
Deserving someone who loves | Adores me
Someone willing | To do the work | Love requires
Someone who enjoys | Both the ease of love
The struggle Love can bring
Someone willing to surrender | To rise up
To the magic | To the relationship before us

"Seeing Clearly," Puerto Rico

Dancing Demons

I'm dancing with my demons

Words emoting from my mouth | Causing my body

To physically move | Shaking their presence

Loose from | A familiar hangout

Jumping and moving | No longer

Swinging in | Causing chaos

Laughingly swinging out

I'm coming alive

No longer afraid | Calling them out

With honesty | With truth

They willingly come | Knowing ultimately

They are under my command

Created by me | Crafted by me

Kept alive by me

They are alive

In me

No more are they allowed to live

To thrive within | They've been called

To the banquet table | Put in their place

The Light of Love | Shined brightly

Into their eyes | No longer

Needed within

No longer

Having

A welcomed home

I'm becoming
    Me
        The real Me
           The one
               Thrown into
                   The Universe
                       At the beginning
                          The brave one
                             Fighting for

Every scrap
Every breath
Every freedom
The one and only... Me

Truth

Truth is truth

But is it?

More than a chemical | Stripping away the dream
Tearing apart | The hope
Ripping into the desire | Often making **truth** tellers
The enemy | Someone and something | To avoid
To dismiss | To separate from

My journey | Into the Light
Out from the Dark | Allowing me
To come closer | To the **truth**
Removing lies | Old stories
Being disassembled | Like a bomb
Found unspent | A UXO (unexploded ordinance)

My **truth** telling | Becoming a stronger part
Of who | I really am
"The **truth** shall set you free"
Words spoken from the lips of Jesus
Do we really want the freedom
*Found by walking through the **truth**?*
Set loose from the very desires we hold on so tightly too?
*Do we want to walk the dark path that the **truth** demands?*

The mirror | Serving to call us first
Discovering our **truth** | Before ever
Calling upon | **Truth** | To find another

I choose to walk | Within the shadow | Of the **Truth**
To be | A **truth-bearer** | Truly at any cost

Walk with me...

"No Bullshit," NCAR Trail, Boulder Colorado

Artistry

For some it's canvas | For others it's brick walls | While some
Play on stage | Dancing openly to the music
Internally and externally
My art | Is relationship
Fluid movement | Hidden notes | A symphony
Unseen by most | Connecting pieces
Serving as | A glazier | Filling in cracks | Stepping in
Gently pursuing
Understanding the gaps | Are where | Love | True Love
Can be | Easily lost | Or so beautifully found
My hands are my brush | Lovingly caressing
Serving others | Empathy guiding | A reservoir of experiences
Thousands of stories | Pulling from
My ink | My paint
Love is | Given freely | Barriers removing | Fully capable Explicitly
real | Constantly alive | In the moment | No longer
Allowing fear | Holding back | The rush | Of fluid warmth
My dance | Interpretation through | Intimacy and kindness
Allowing movement | Serving within | Me | My first Love
The Spirit | Intertwining Universe | Surrendering within
Loves purest embrace
Shame | Anger | Codependency | Self-hatred
Slowly leaving | Liquid healing
Replacing pain's tentacles
Deepest of wounds | Leaving like a thorn

Being pushed outward | By a finger's desire | For freedom
Dancing within the knowing
My art | My artistry | Becoming more | Than enough

"Layers of Beauty," Cork & Coffee Highlands,
Denver, Colorado

RHYTHMIC DNA

She moves me   Her rhythm

B   d
e   r
a   u
t   m
i   s
n
g
drums   From the beginning of time

Her Love   The sticky glue   Holding together

Every first breath   Ever breathed
Within existence

She is perfection   A movement

A flow   A dance   Causing my DNA

Our DNA   To fully come alive

She is in every movement   Every step

Intertwining existence   Within Her

Loving embrace

She captures every color   Within Her illustrious eyes

Because of Her beauty   We have beauty

Because of Her Divinity   We can glimpse

The Divine

Because of Her warmth   We are warmed

Because…

"Her Flow," Jon Huerta in Highlands, Denver, Colorado

Given

Rumi speaks so clearly
"So much is given in the receiving"
I've heard his quotes spoken | Many times
Over the past weeks | The essence of these words
Washing over me | Through me | In a tidal wave
Of pure Light

Love's kiss | Embalming me | The intoxicating fragrance
Flowing forth | From every | Opening pores
Forever changing | Forever changed

The boomerang effect | Of receiving kindness
Giving kindness | Of seeing | And being seen
Empathy's gentle hug | Rising forth | The ease
Of trust's weight | Mutually surrendering | Not allowing
Fear's embrace | To take hold | Living within | The fiery hug
Brought forth | By the sacred moment | Scorched by demons
Haunted by shame | Hunted with regret | Surviving through
 Courageously stepping | Again and again
Onto the battleground | For the freedom | So immensely
Sought after | Giving and receiving | Echoing words | To live
Being loved

Within their gentle embrace

Circles

I've been circling | My entire life
Thinking | No believing
I'm somehow free | From the circle
I believe | I've taken | A right turn in a maze
Of left turns | Yet | I end up
Back at | The same place | Each time
Every time wondering
What the hell happened?
Funny how | Now that I've surrendered
To the process | The circles | Are now
Disappearing from sight | Being replaced
With a new circle | One that holds
No boundaries | Bountifully embracing
Me
The me | That is
Not that should be
Allowing me to let go | Of the circle
The one | With the fortress walls
Holding me in | Holding me down
I open | Moving in an infinite wondering
Allowing the path | To call me home
Immersed in the past
Excited for the future
Grounded within
The glorious moment

"Circling Innocence," Julius Breckling Riverfront Park,
Little Rock, Arkansas

Dressed in White

My dream
Waking me up | Furiously writing
Hauntingly delightful | *She was dressed in white*
From head to toe | We were playing | A wonderful game
Of flirting delight | Witnessing her | Self-love | Seeing mine
In her reflection | My gaze setting her | On fire | Her moving
Causing my deep well | Of desire | To bubble over
Only words spoken | Within giggles | Of pure delight
Not knowing | Exactly what | She desired
Until I knew | Gently laying down | Opening herself
To me | Her elegant body | Shining like | The brightest star
Blinding me in love | The loveliest of lovely | Perfectly shining
Her openness and desire | To know me | To be known
Causing an ancient | Stirring within |Tears of longing
Bursting forth

As I first met her | Flowing gracefully | Amongst stars above
Her sighs of delight | Dancing Intertwining DNA
Bringing forth | Childlike laughter | From us both
Celebrating the beauty | Of being found | Of being home
Home within | Home with another | Home safely cocooned
Within this juicy embrace

She's inviting me | Deeper within | Wanting me

209

No needing me | To know | All of her | The invitation
Taking my breath away | Causing a stirring | Felt from
Timelines of old | My warrior | Dancing around the fire

My Vi-King | Running into the fire | Serving my Vi-Queen
My King | King Richard | Meeting her | My Queen
Creating safety

Everything I was
Everything I am
Everything I will be
Stepping | No diving | Deep into
Her pool of light | Her garden of delight | Inviting her
The translucent Queen | To rise | Taking her place
In love
In grace
In beauty
Raising the chalice together | The eruption
Taking us | Running through the halls
Of 1,000 years | Making it home | AGAIN…

"Translucent Wings," Adams County Historical Museum,
Brighton, Colorado

FOUND IN THE ECHO

Echoes of Love
  Rebounding violently
Bursting through

Unfelt chapters
  Desiring towards
The sun

Glimmering Light
  Bursting within
Slowly creeping forward

Seen
Yet
Unseen

Moving into
  The cracks
Broken shards

Welcoming into

Exposed skin
  Causing unseen pain
Unseen longing

Searching to
  Be seen
Smothered within
  The loss

Felt
  yet
Unfelt

Welcoming in
  Loves gentle breath
Breathing new
  Into the old

The echo

The new

Becoming old

The old

Becoming new

Refreshing renewal

Childlike awe

Adult wonder

Intertwining DNA

Slowly becoming

The reborn
Me

"Echo in Silence," Porto Ceresio, Italy

Richard Lee Ellsmore

The chapters | Of Richard Lee Ellsmore
Being lovingly brought | Further into the light
Each page | Being carefully pursued | And read
Gently inviting me | To step further | Into Me | All of me
Starting with the delight | Heard first from a UK accent
"You are a Richard" | "At least to me" | Not knowing
What to think
At first | And now | Looking forward to hearing
My given name | The one I have hated | My whole life through
Affecting everything
Every area | Every inch
Chapters | Stories | Hidden away
In the dark | Being coaxed out
Like a wounded dog | Chained up | Underneath a porch
Gently unhooked | Welcomed into Love
The healing salve | Of Love
Inviting me deeper | Into freedom's embrace
To the Sacred Home | Within
Cuddling Me | As I am
As I am becoming

"Loving Hand," Highlands, Denver, Colorado

Unrequited

Damien Rice's "The Blower's Daughter" was playing when I wrote this poem.

A love
One that has no need | For a response
One that admires
Deeply appreciates | Without a reply
My eyes only on you
Such a beauty | In just loving | The feeling
Owning deeply within
An understanding | That it might | Not be returned
Allowing this
To be okay
To truly love | Is to release
To allow freedom | To choose
Or not choose | Longing for
The choose | To be chosen
Choosing life | Together
Knowing either way | Never to be
The same

Find A God Who Likes You

Stick to Your Guns's "Life in a Box" was playing when I wrote this poem.

Does your God like you?
I recently heard a song asking this question

I've been camping | On this idea
These past few weeks | Rebounding back
Into a place | Of wondering

Why are we taught that God doesn't really like us?
Why do we stay with that destructive view of ourselves?

I'm stretching | I've stretched | Into the beyond
A place | I never fully knew | I could get to
One that includes | And expanding view | Of God
Whomever He and She | Really is

Understanding that I | That we are Love
That God | Spirit | Essence
Lives within | Is in | Is us
While I am not | Making decisions

For the world | I am | Part of the fabric
That is
The One
The Way
The Truth
The Life
The Light
That brightens | Every crevice
Every millimeter | Of this world
Including all others

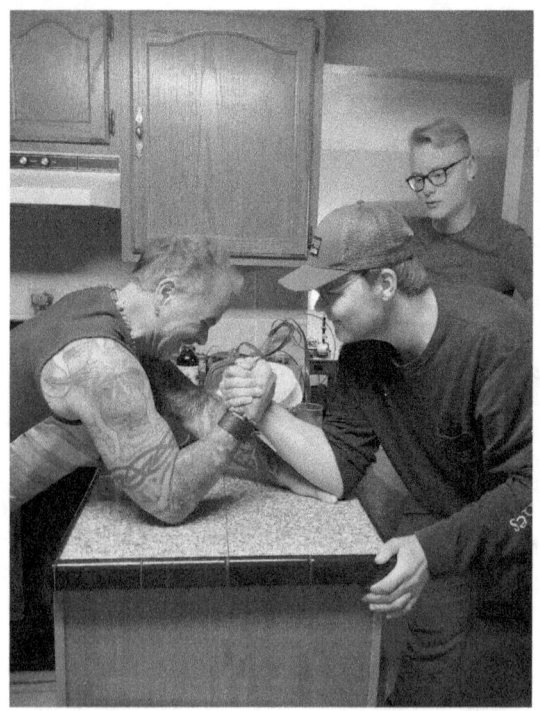

*"Wrestling," My sons, Jake and Mitchell (I'm arm wrestling),
in Westminster, Colorado*

GIVING
OF FEAR

⊢────⊣

Hiding my fears
Well, I became an expert
The houses | The communities
I grew up within | A necessary | Means of survival

Locking away | All emotion | The punishment
For not doing so | A steep slide | Into pain's sting
The life-long scar | Reminding me | The consequences
Of emotions

The hiding | Of me | Forcing myself
Into a grown-up shell | At such a young age
Feeling old | Being a 12-year-old boy

In many ways | At 54-years-young
Starting again | Choosing | A different way
The Way

Allowing fear | A place | At my table
One overflowing | With emotion | Steeped within
The Love | Of the moment

Childlike in it's joy
Overflowing in wonder
Cocooned within | The awe
Of being found |By Love

Two Wonderful-S

Visualizing you
Walking back   Walking forward
Following a way
    An ancient way | Old but new | Back to your true essence
       Walking deeper | Into the light | Reclaiming you
         Your spirit | Your fire | Picking items up
           Not new things | Old items
             Things you | Have used
           In the past | Familiar in | Your hand
        Putting them | In your pocket |
     Comforting you | Wrapping you | In their embrace
Reaching deeper | Into the earth | The weight
Of that act | Bringing such peace | The audible | Slow breath
   Bringing it | Deeper within
     Your essence | The breath carrying
       You into | Your future | Present now
         The you that | Was held down
           Held back | May you
           Have the courage
             To continue
            To walk into
         That new | Old you
       My desire | Is to encourage
     To help | Getting there | When needed
   No shackling | Holding back | Serving you

In this call | This journey | Serving you
Within this | Higher calling | Given to each other
As a gift | So clear | Walking deeper
Into our destiny | Walking both
Backwards and forward | Balancing
Growing together
Warrior-ing together
Building a fortress
Of us

No man
No woman
No establishment
No fear
Can tear down

You have brought | With you | SO much joy
Joy | So, so deep
No words |Unable to speak
Words unable | To do justice | To the feeling
Ohhh sweet one | Oh my god
Thank you | Thank you
It's because | Of you
Not you
How wild
Is that | It is us | It is me
It is you | Magic together
Uncontrollable | But yet | In control
Speeding up | Slowing down
Saying yes | Saying no

The littlest-est | Of change

Reflecting this | Massive change

Never having love | Being this free

It is incredible | Allowing me

Sharing places

Full experiences

Never shared before

Sharing what | I see | Feel

I disappear | Into moments | Just happening

In that moment | Completely lost

Loving | Every millisecond | At peace

New peace | Never felt | Experienced before

Wonderful you | Wonderful us |

Two wonderful-S

Coming together | Creating

Most wonderful

Vibrating alive | Shaking loose

Old ghosts

New Love's kiss

You have me

More of me | Every day

Presently present | Into whatever

This is | Whatever this will be

"Burning Bush," Westminster, Colorado

Never... (Ever) Enough

"When" versus now
"Should be" versus are
"Can't" versus will try

When you are *stable*
When you are *rich*
When you are *better*
When you are *whole*
When you are *healed*
When you are *more*
When you are *equal*
When you *measure up*

As you are | You are not enough
Words I've heard | Sometimes spoken
Always implied
Words I see | Clearly feeling
Imprinted upon | My soul
Yours as well love
I speak to myself | To you | My beloved
You are enough
Because you are | You
Caring

Beautiful
Lovely
You

You | As you are | Exactly where | Exactly who
You are | To be | As am I

You are | So much more | Than you even believe
Or understand | Yourself to be
As am I

You are made | To love | To be loved
I've experienced this | Am experiencing
It more | With every day
Every Conversation spoken | Written and unwritten
With you

I've got you
Words I wrote | As the reality | Is setting in
You have me | As I have you | Able to hold
You and me | The foundation stretching
But holding

We hold | We continue
Never enough | No more
More than enough | WE are

May the ink | Of the spoken words
Become disappearing ink
Dissolving into LOVE

UNIVERSE POURING

|—————|

Masculine   into   feminine

Feminine   into   Masculine

Awakening into higher

Divinity afoot

Dancing delightful DNA

Connecting us into and through

The Divine

Into the Trilogy | 1+1+3

You and me… becoming

Melting into | Separate but yet

Alive-er within

Willingly poured | Embraced and seen

Beauty surrounding | Shining beyond

Into the Infinite | Into the Beloved

Joy's expanse | Being seen

Witnessing Sacred

Inviting blinding

Hallowed kiss | Each unique strand

Gamboling alive

Within Sacred DNA

Embracing Love | Twirling across | The liquid Love

In sheer enchanting ecstasy

RLove

Feeling

RDivine

"Dancing DNA," Highlands in Denver, Colorado

Hallowed Hall

Desire growing and fluid
Water pouring upon ink
Flowing down nourishing
Rising into fire, into us
The art of you dancing alive
Vividly seeing inward beauty
Inviting into waterfalls of delight
Inner sanctuary, Hallowed Halls
Reverence silencing words
Touch and reflecting free eyes only
Compass needle drawing us deeper
Following the sacred inviting
Leading onward into the wild unknown
The forest floor inviting sensory overload
Her spell simultaneously causing surrender and delight

"Banquet Hall," Trek Hostel, Ghent, Belgium

Dancing with Desire

His illustrious flow
  Divinity masculine | Drawing me deeper within
    Causing a stir deeper and richer
      Then ever experienced before
        My eternal roots rising up | Where in the past
      They would shrink back
    In revolt, revolted by fear
  Fearing true desire | The taught language
  Desire is wrong, bad, destructive
  Masculinity must live within blinders
Beauty impossible to be appreciated without
  Her feminine wiles consuming
    Enslaving to inward desire, to sin
      Acting out | Seducing ways
        No more! | A revolting Essence within
          Accepting a new reality
            One birthing from above and below
              Roots and Light abound
                Slowly removing the
                  Poisoned words
                    In its place fresh knowing
                      One built upon the Eternal
                    and Sacred
                  Allowing for true desire
                Tasting Her upon His lips

Inviting Love's touch
The true flow behind Desire
One built not upon selfishly consuming
Building into surrendering
Sacrificing, rising up
Into their love-ing embrace
Hallows eve
Desire the welcome mat
To the Sacred True

"Flaming" Elizabeth, Colorado

Getting Into Reality

JJ Grey & Mofro's "Lochloosa (Live)" was playing when I wrote this poem.

Walking within Her | I feel it
No, I experience it | No, I live it
I go there to | Find my reality
Curling up in | Those loving arms
Snuggling skin to skin | Feeling Her breath
Upon my skin

Calling me back | Into the reality
Of true peace | Joy's illustrious smile
Causing a skip | Uncontrollable body movement
Every little detail | A stream's drip
Upon the rocks | Squirrels dancing in delight
Racing upon the Pines | Fresh snow melting off
Bendy Aspen limbs

Every little micro movement | A call
One heard only | To those willing | To listen
The sound of | True silence | Found within
The silence | Alive within the silence
Echoing a calling | Well done
My good and faithful lover

Welcome to the | Truest of desire
The pleasure found in peace
The real | Found within **real-it**-y
The real *it* | Discovered only
Living into the now

FINALLY HOME

The Odyssey *by Symphony X was playing when I wrote this poem.*

Home | He finally made it home
The power | Exquisite vocals
Depth of words | Inviting me current
Into a life | Being fully lived
Allowing the sweet nectar | Of enticing home
To draw me in | A bear to honey

I have survived the stings
The uncontrollable storm
Washing me up | Upon Her shores
Again and again
Tenacity's scratchy embrace | Calling me back
Out to sea | Setting sail
Destination unknown | The course set
Refusing to live in reverse

Home | Discovering home within
Sharing home | My home
The warmth | Coming forth from my hearth
With a lovely precious one

"Wonderful World," Sunset Park, Westminster, Colorado

ABOUT THE AUTHOR

Rick is a survivor. He even has the word *tenacity* tattooed on his body. His life started in the Alaska wilderness sandwiched between the mountains and the sea. While the beauty of eagles, grizzly bears, and salmon-filled rivers served as a backdrop, his family life was filled with fear, shame, and the loneliness found in being a "missed" child. Because of the abuses suffered outside and within his home Rick created and lived within survival shell into adulthood.

The last twenty-five years Rick has spent redefining himself through a painful process of tearing down the old foundation and building a new one on a freshly discovered love for self and others. Counselors, coaches, mentors, self-help books, seminars, and retreats have all added to this trail he has walked, but ultimately it has been through the love of close friends, and his time alone in nature that has brought forth this new person.

The real Rick, coming out as RLove, now lives within the gorgeous moments given within every day. It's inside words that he has continued to discover the true meaning of love and beauty. It's within daily hand-to-hand combat with his own self-hatred, and loathing that he has discovered the inner peace that's been sought out for his entire life.

Along the way, he has worked many jobs, has lived in many diverse places, has started traveling the world, has found and lost lovers, has made friends with a wide range of people, and continues to be a father to three sons. These three young men, all over twenty-one, serve as a guiding point on the compass. They humble him and call him back to the reality of how amazing, and difficult these most important relationships can be.